BUSINESS OUTSOURCING STRATEGIES

JOHN LOK

Copyright © John Lok
All Rights Reserved.

This book has been published with all efforts taken to make the material error-free after the consent of the author. However, the author and the publisher do not assume and hereby disclaim any liability to any party for any loss, damage, or disruption caused by errors or omissions, whether such errors or omissions result from negligence, accident, or any other cause.

While every effort has been made to avoid any mistake or omission, this publication is being sold on the condition and understanding that neither the author nor the publishers or printers would be liable in any manner to any person by reason of any mistake or omission in this publication or for any action taken or omitted to be taken or advice rendered or accepted on the basis of this work. For any defect in printing or binding the publishers will be liable only to replace the defective copy by another copy of this work then available.

Copyright

All rights reserved. This book or any portion thereof may not be
reproduced or used in any manner whatsoever without the express
written permission of the publisher except for the use of brief quotations
in a
book review or scholarly journal.

Contents

Preface

Although, nowadays, outsourcing is popular strategy to any global organizations. But they neglect outsourcing strategy has also disadvantages to some organizational departments. This book concerns to explain why outsourcing strategy can bring benefits to some organizational departments, but it can also bring disadvantages to some organizational departments.

I shall indicate evidences to explain what the reasons are not right when the organizations choose outsourcing strategy to some departments as well as what the reasons are right when the organizations choose outsourcing strategy to other departments. It is suitable to any students who have interest to research outsourcing strategy.

This book brings readers image yourselves are organizational outsourcing strategic professionals. You need to help your organizational different departments to implement outsource strategy. In this outsourcing strategy journey, you will feel what positive or negative influences when your outsouring implementation period.

Prologue

Table of contents

CHAPTER ONE

ORGANIZATIONAL OUTSOURCING STRATEGY

Information Technology Outsourcing

Information technology outsourcing advantages

In any organization information technology department, information system operations remain the predominant function outsourced, other functions are also being performed by external service providers and the relationship is between outsourcing and certain demographics: size, industry is formation intensity. The results suggest that system operations remain being performed by external service providers. Further, industry and information intensity has some influence on the extent of outsourcing of certain functions.

Information technology department outsoucring benefits may include as below:

The first reason is cost reduction, trying to remain competitive and up-to-date is becoming a financial burden to many organizations. This is true particularly in fields, such as banking and financial services, health care and manufacturing. Hiring outsiders to handle part or even all of its information system often helps an organization to provide better services and maintain a competitive advantage. The information technology industry choice of outsourcing factor is related to size, industry type and information technology.

The second reason is technological and/or human resources in the management of the information technology infrastructure skill improvement. The information technology department outsourcing service to external service provider, includes the degree of internalization of technological resources and the degree of internalization of human resources. Some economists defined internalization of outsourcing service is as ownership is by the focal organization which takes on full control with profit and loss responsibility. Also who define outsourcing is as involving a significant use of resources, either technological and/or human resources, external to the organizational hierarchy in the management of the information technology infrastructure.

So the information technology external service providers includes: applications development and maintenance, systems operations, networks/ telecommunications management and user computing support, system planning and management purchase of application software, but excludes business consulting services, after-sale vendor services and the lease of telephone lines etc. outsourcing services.

The third reason is economics of scale in areas of hardware, software. This pressure is seen as the most significant factor driving today's corporate interest. An outsourcing service provision might be in a position to exploit economics of scale in areas of hardware, software and staff since it pools different kind of technological projects from many service receivers. Outsourcing information technological service can reduce the corporate's cost with the high level of IT investment, there are increasing pressures to move away from fixed expenditure, corporate overhead towards a more direct variable cost approach to control the IT operations.

The IT costs can become predictable for overruns is often placed on the service provider. Outsourcing service can allow the service to gain immediate access to competitiveness in delivering products or services as well as to avoid of obsolescence risk, due to the changes in the nature of the IT infrastructure, the risk of obsolescence is high. Outsourcing can allow the service provider has the ability to diversify these risks across a broad range of service receivers. However, long term contracts might in spread the risk, the weakness is back to the receiver.

It seems outsourcing IT service has also these disadvantages: such as, loss of flexibility or managerial control. Outsourcing reduces real or perceived control over both quality real or perceived control over both the quality of software and the timetable of project since the work is now being carried out by people not under direct supervision.

It also threats to long term career prospects to information system professionals because many of them do not find suitable. Is jobs or promising career paths in both areas of the corporation. Outsourcing also increases coordination cost.

It may requires increasing time to communicate and coordinate with the service provider. Traditionally, the formal meeting cost of negotiating and monitoring the outsourcing contract are potentially wide ranging, indirect and substantial increasing, such as, additional releasing or transferring employees, in license transfer by software vendors and in re-negotiating contracts costs. So, the IT industry of profit motivates service provider might not be in the least interests of the outsourcing service receivers. Some IT service providers are in the business of maximizing their profit at any cost, this could run counter to a service receiver's interest.

Human resource outsourcing

2.1 Outsourcing or insourcing in human resource supply chain factor

To choosing of outsourcing or insourcing in human resource supply chain factor of the controlling service demanders needs to concern this issues: Should human resource activities be provided in house or should all or past of those activities be outsourced? The relationship between organizational structure and the HR function is an important variable. The individual activities that comprise HR systems include not only the employee life cycle from recruiting to termination, but also planning for organizational staffing needs and improving organizational effectiveness.

How organizations need to outsource HR function to not care employees knowledge and skill is a factor to influence any organizations choose to outsourcing non core employees when which have no any right employees to be promoted to do the position. For example, firms engage in HR outsourcing to reduce management access HR expertise, achieve workforce flexibility, focus managerial resources and keep up with changing workplace negotiations. Also, supporting the tend is the availability of common technology platform, which can reduce costs for organizations and risks.

However, organizations are afraid of losing some control over delivery of outsourcing services and finding themselves dependent on the vendor or liable for the vendors actions where there are both benefits and challenges may be informed by the structure of the relationship between client firms and these organizations offering the outsourced activities to client firms.

What variables are impacted by HR outsourcing of staffing? Which include: administrative costs for labor expense, client firm to HR relations, HR regulatory competency requirement, knowledge of cost factors, e.g. billing and pay rates, vendor markups and margins, vendor management competency requirement, client and vendor relationship, communication is between client managers and staffing vendor, employee data-available, data quality control, data security, match with job requirement, employee quality, inter-vendor competition, mining of client talent by vendor , quality content for preferred staffing vendor, standardization of business process (intra-company), strategic focus of client firm, demands on client managers vendor competency and external economic environmental viability.

However, it has dynamic relationship between the client firms and staffing vendors. Moreover, the models of human resource supply chain, every has different set of advantages and disadvantages for the client firms. The models can be relate to the decision making process on outsourcing of human resources. As strategic services tactic decisions have an important impact or selecting the particular HR outsourcing model that a client firm adopter.

The another model is the balance of power and control over managing the control workers differ to decide what every worker individual skills or abilities outsourcing demand. Moreover, local contracting is also the predominant traditional model for outsourcing staffing with non-core employees. A client firm usually uses several staffing vendors to meet temporary staffing needs for seasonal functions, employee absences and special projects. The advantages of local contracting are high touch and high quality of service by staffing vendors, minimal bureaucracy, empowerment of hiring any high qualified employees to get the job done, and a relatively better fit between specific staffing vendors and functional needs.

2.1 The disadvantages of local contracting

The disadvantages of local contracting can increase costs from non-standardization of hiring practices and procedures across the client form, a significant amount of word of mouth and subjective quality issues, high local costs and client firm us subjected to the capabilities of the staffing vendors and contract employees. However, local HR contracting is the most flexible, high quality, but expense, inefficient and ineffective HR outsourcing model for the client firm. Another model is the working period to be decided to outsource HR contracting. In this situation, in the short term and on a day-to-day basis, the client firm aims to achieve on economy of scale with its staffing vendors. The total costs of temporary workers as well as internal costs for contracting with several different vendors are higher than if it needs one staffing vendors to meet all its needs. So, the client company can set the reasonable pricing that it pays for its temporary outsourcing staffs. Each staffing vendor secures a different rate range with each vendor as opposed as one contact. In the long term, it is benefiting, each specialized staffing vendor is able to fully work with each function needs temporary utilization is better than the average. Mismatches are fewer. Functional departments are able to receive a high quality / high touch service in any time period. Another model is the centralizing is when the department standardizes the staffing process to drive costs down of temporary workers. This tends to occur when a percentage of non-core employees reach a certain ratio of core employees. The advantages include more uniform standards in hiring process, billing rates and pay rates, departmental hiring managers can refocus their effort to choose outsourcing staffing, criteria may be established for a performed suppliers list and greater security for the staffing established vendors that offer higher quality services. The disadvantages include new departmental responsibilities in HR which decreases outsourcing efficiencies for the organizations daily administrative direction is rather than long term strategic direction. Usually lacking qualifications to fulfill the responsibilities, overall, centralizing of HR outsourcing is that firms can achieve more standardization which additional bureaucratic costs and the necessary non-core jobs do not get done as a need. Another model is purchasing HR, which manages staffing vendors from HR to the purchasing unit of an organizations. The goal is to continue cost reductions by increasing efficiencies. In conclusion, the main benefits of HR outsourcing include maintaining organizational control over the hiring process, application of purchasing capabilities for greater standardization in hiring processes pay rates and bill rates. So, any outsoucred HR organizations may be reduce hiring process cost.

Valus supply chain outsourcing

Global outsourcing source strategy in a value supply chain advantages

What is global outsourcing source strategy in a departmental role? In a highly competitive global environment, many manufacturers are responded by setting and outsourcing relations for components and finished products with lower cost producers on a contractual electronic commerce department, (original equipment manufacturer basis). Outsourcing strategy is part of the value supply chain of corporate activated. Nowadays, global outsourcing increases organizational and technological capacity of firms and cooperating a network of remotely located external suppliers performing.

These understanding the important roles that product designers, engineers and production managers and purchasing manager etc. play in global sourcing strategy empowerment. Specially, electronic commerce is popular to supply chain. For example, Toyota car manufacturing company, owns unique capabilities by designing and manufacturing certain car components in-house , i.e. insourcing. Toyota also outsource manufacturing activities, Toyota adopts purchasing necessary, but no strategic inputs from independent component suppliers on obtaining a lower cost for these inputs. For example, products would be belts, tires and batteries to vehicle products that are not customized and do not differentiate its products from its competitors. Toyota's outsourcing strategy is car strategic inputs provide differentiation, e.g. engine, transmission etc. are sources from suppliers based on strategic partnership to gain to access to suppliers' capabilities and it is also a conceptualize global outsourcing sourcing strategy to Toyota car manufacturing company.

How value chain outsourcing affects firm level performance. Global outsourcing strategy means to identify which production units that will serve which particular markets and how components will be supplied for production and thus included a number of basic choices, companies can make in decision how to serve various markets. Either choice relates to the use of inputs, assembly or production within the country to serve a foreign market or decides to use of internal or external supplies of components or finished products. In this outsourcing source input situation, the term sourcing is needed to describe how multi-national companies mange in of components and finished products in serving foreign and domestic markets. Sourcing decision making is both contractual point of view, the sourcing of major components and products are occurred by multi-national companies. First is from parents or their foreign subsidiaries. Second is from independent suppliers on a contractual basis. The first type of sourcing is known as insourcing. Otherwise, the second type of sourcing is referred to outsourcing. How to achieve economies of scale by outsourcing or insourcing sourcing input strategy? Therefore, the two outsourcing strategies are multi-faceted and require careful examination.

The two economists (Abrahamson & Rosenkopf, 1993) indicated that In long term, outsourcing can help to reduce fixed investment in finance view point, in-house manufacturing facilities and thus lower the breakeven point, which subsequently helps boost an outsourcing company whose return on equity (ROE). Thus, if any one corporate performance is evaluated on the basis of its contribution to the company's ROE.

Also, in the short term or long term on resource inputs outsourcing view, early adopters of outsourcing strategy indeed experienced efficiency gains as they were able to reduce fixed investment in in-house manufacturing facilities and lows their ROE. But, later adopters may have different to gain institutions legitimacy or because of competition pressures in the industry, despite some inherent uncertainties about the long term costs and benefits of outsourcing strategy. It seems that outsourcing strategy was devised as any organization's policy makers to access trade linkages of benefits for short term or long term.

Outsourcing strategy is a systematic analysis of the economic, political and regulatory implications indicates potential benefits along with a number of potentially negative side effects to any organizations. Then, outsourcing strategy will be caused this question: How to assess the risks and benefits of outsourcing for organizational sectors and nations both? The decision to change outsourcing behavior to carry a business activity may have profound implications for outsourcer and outsource receiver both, but little impact of the sector level. The common occurrence of industry decisions to outsource most manufacturing, including sale of factories, it created a new sub-sector, contract manufacturing. Otherwise, at a national level and public sectors become less distinct to outsourcing strategy. Public policy on outsourcing has stimulated extensive debate, privatization social justice and value for money etc. challenges.

What is environmental uncertainty factor?

4.1 What motivate outsourcing what is being outsourced risk and concerns?

Whether what motivate outsourcing, evidence of what is being outsourced risk and concerns? Outsourcing activities include: outsources manufacturing components and other value adding activities. Some focused on employment is outsourced another firm's employees carrying out tasks previously performed one's own employees. Outsourcing is an activity outside the organization's chosen core competencies. It seems outsourcing is a sub-contracting relationships between firms, all foreign production, hiring of workers in non-traditional jobs, such as control workers and temporary and part time workers.

What are the motivations for outsourcing reasons? Why outsourcing is needed to any organization. For example, it can enable firms to focus on core activities. The concept of focus originates in operation on a small, manageable, number of tasks at which the operation becomes excellent to specific technologies and as a risk of vertical integration advantages. Other benefits of outsourcing appear is literature on strategic management, operations management, purchasing and supply and innovations. Moreover, outsourcing can improve flexibility to meet changing business conditions, demands for products, services and technologies by creating smaller and more flexible clear evidence includes improved creditability image, greater workforce flexibility and avoiding being backed into specific assets and technologies are harder to measure. How outsourcing can improve company performance. For airline manufacturing industry example, Hill & Jones (1995) showed that the manufacture of a large portion of the Boeing 767 is Boeing's third largest commercial aircraft, which is outsourced to Japanese manufacturers, which include Fuji, Kawasaki and Mitsubish. As a result, only 10% of the value of the 767 Boeing is produced in-house. So, outsourcing is an attempt to enhance manufacturing air place industry competitiveness.

How can choose smarter outsourcing? Organizations hope to do sight options to save money, among themselves staff layoffs and a reduction of overhead costs, such as office space. Private companies have long outsourced in order to save time and money. During periods of economic growth, many organizations began to use outsourcing more frequently and staff workloads grew in proportion to increase budgets. Tasks such as conducting needs assessments, reviewing proposals, conducting site visits, monitoring and creating evaluations systems were increasingly given to outside contractors, consulting firms and independent consultants in the belief that external specialists could do the work more efficiently and effectively than company itself.

Nowadays, there is a growing stream of organizations need to research into the outsourcing of innovation activities within the innovation, management, marketing and economics disciplines. These organizations need to understand how with the outsourcing practice becoming more commonplace in their industry. However, their behaviors bring these two questions: Whether outsource or internalize innovation activities and the performance implications of this decision can support for both transaction cost and resource based arguments is examined with both theory bases showing substantial attention?

Whether outsourcing innovation activities can lead to faster product development and cost savings? On advantages hand, it is possible that outsourcing may lead to higher costs and slower new product development. Further the technological uncertainty may have conflicting impacts on the outsourcing decision that are not yet well understand. When outsourcing product development has reduced costs and has proved speed to market. On disadvantages hand, outsourcing has also reduce product development time delays and higher quality concerns. Why to cause performance implications of outsourced innovation activities in transaction in cost economics and the resource-based view point? When outsourcing product development has been to reduce costs and has improved speed to market, outsourcing product development is not unlike other make or buy decisions. So, make vs buy decision is similar to logistic and IT outsourcing. Internalization of product development will be preferred when transaction costs are excessive. Otherwise, the market i.e. outsourcing will be selected when transaction costs are low. Transaction costs can include adaption, safeguarding and measurement costs. Adaption costs represent efforts to adjust contract to change conditions and are a result of environmental uncertainty.

When a firm may have to revise on agreement with a partner company, this facing substantial penalties, due to an unstable market environments, the firm is likely to perform this function internally. Safeguarding costs characterize the costs of an outsourcing provider acting opportunities after investments have been made in the inter-firm relationship and are the result of transaction specific investment. Measurement costs include all expenses with confirming that contracts have been fulfilled passably. The contracting firm may face substantial costs to estimate quality for contractual services. When the sum total of these transaction costs is substantial, internalization will be favored.

4.2 What is environmental uncertainty factor?

Environmental uncertainty refers to unanticipated changes in circumstances surrounding an exchange in market uncertain and technological uncertainty. Market uncertainty is the fluctuation and unpredictability of demand. With respect to innovation projects, market uncertainty may cause frequent changes to the development, complications and adding expense to external contracting. These changes may necessitate renegotiation or cancellation of innovation contracts, which will likely carry prohibitive penalties (a term) transaction costs. These transaction costs promote internalization under high levels of market uncertainty. Otherwise, technological uncertainty environments, selecting market governance allows firms the flexibility to end relationship should technical requirements shift. It seems that market and technological external change factor will influence to benefits to any organizations to choose outsourcing strategy. On the other side, outsourcing can bring this question: Whether the offshore outsourcing of information technology jobs choice is suitable to any IT organizations? Nowadays. The offshore outsourcing if IT jobs from the United States has been enabled by a powerful influence of global economic demographic and technological forces. In fact, many IT companies were drawn to offshoring outsourcing because of the need for programmers to fix the Y2K problem in the late 1990- year. It is shortages of US programmers.

Other factors driving this phenomenon include the wage gap between the US and developing countries, e.g. China and India, advances in technology, labor availability, expanding foreign markets and foreign government incentives. The spread of the offshoring phenomenon from low skill manufacturing to high wage white collar service industry jobs reduces the country's IT jobs critics, it represents the mobility for many

US workers who saw post-secondary education as the route to a higher standard of living. The offshoring outsourcing of manufacturing and service jobs from the US to lower cost foreign nations become a national issue in a very short time. The impact of offshore outsource on the information technology sector gives outsourcing potential loss of millions of jobs at all wage levels and the critical contribution is the IT sector to US productivity growth. However, decisions about the locations of manufacturing or service facilities reflect market forces key factors include the size of local markets, capital availability and costs, labor availability skill levels and cost, logistic issues, reliability and infrastructure and IT in particular relationships with research institutions. All these factors will influence the choice of offshore outsource IT jobs strategy top any organizations.

4.3 Whether outsourcing can bring what benefit of work skills

Whether outsourcing will bring what kind of work skills. Many employers choose outsourcing to employ employees. This core of our work is identifying trends which will transform global society and the global marketplace. How it influences our nature of work form health care to technology, the work place and human identity. A decade ago, workers worried about jobs being outsourced overseas. Today companies, such as Odesk and Liveops can assemble teams " in the cloud" to dosales, customer support and many other tasks. It seems outsoucring can influence many high technological job of changes. Global connectivity, smart machines and new media are just some of the drivers reshaping how we thank about work, what constitutes work and the skills, we shall need to be productive contributors in the future. As computer technology in the cloud will be used popularly to society. A signal is typically a small or local innovation that has the potenial to grow in scale and geographic distribution. A signal can be a new product, a new practice, a new market strategy, a new policy or new technology, such as online cloud computing files storage service method. It is an innovative social science method to computer users. However, this new computer files storage method influences outsourcing service of needs increasing. It will have key drivers and skills areas that will be most relevant to the technological workforce of the future.

It is estimates that by 2025 year, the number of Americans over 60 age will increase by 70%. The challenge of an aging population will come. What it means to age, individuals will need to rearrange their approach to their career, family life and education to accommodate their life plan. Increasing, people will work long past 65 age in order to have adequate resources for retirement. Multiple careers will be commplace and lifelong learning to prepare for occupational change will see major growth. To take advantage of this well experienced organizations will have to rethink the traditional career paths in organizations, creating more diversity and flexibility. As the high technological cloud computing storage method is invented. Any organizations can save their files to the central cloud computer storage system website to save or find their files from website more easily. It will reduce their computer department expenditure and staff salary. So, outsourcing computer file storage service demands will be influenced to increase to any organizations as well as organizations will reorganize their computer department job nature to shape the kinds of social, economic and political organizations which inhabit. Outsourcing is a good solve method to assist organizations to pay cheap salary to employ many retired high age workers by contract or temporary or part time method to reduce their computer department's number of employees and the retired labors only need to pay cheap salary to learn how to use internet to help whose employers to save their files to their outsourcing computer storage service provider's central computer storage system every day efficiently.

So, organizations do not need to employ many computer department staffs to avoid to pay much salaries to this computer department expenditure. They can choose outsourcing to pay cheap salaries to employ many retirement labors to assist them to do simple office storage job from internet channel efficiently and effectively. Hence, internet high technological innovation can influence office outsoucing of job duties increasing.

Whether domestic outsoucing in the America, what assesses trends and effects on job quality. Nowadays, US firms' use of contractors and independent contractors and its effect on job quality and inequality. Why firms choose contract out for certain functions and assess their predictions about likely impacts on job quality, stagnant wages, growing inquality and the deterioration of job quality are among the most important challenges facing the US economy today. Although any country's domestic outsourcing , firms' use of contractors, franchises and independent contractors any one of these factors is a potentially important influence to companies reduce compensation and shift economy risk to workers. However, the domestic outsoucing takes place on a much larger scale and effects many more workers than has been recognized ranging from low wage service workers, security guards, warehouse workers and hotel housekeepers to professionals and technical workers, such as programmers, health care technicians and accountants. These tends are part of structural change in the organization of production to influence quality of jobs and the nature of employment contract after outsourcing jobs are popular. The quality of jobs include wages, benefits, employee skills and training and mobility opportunities and job security as well as inequality across jobs. Domestic outsoucing concerns these issues: such as employment and labor law, the provision of health, pension and other workplace benefits. However, any companies choose outsourcing of employment reasons include, such as that it relates how management choices to pursue value added or cost focused strategies. Contracting out is difficult to define because a large part ot economic activity has always occurred through business-to-business transactions, as captured in macro-economic input-output models. Outsoucing job employment method can influence any one labor's individual quality of jobs. Usually, international companies choose the offshoring of work in global supply chains. Until recently, the domestic counterpart outsourcing employment method has grown supply chains to domestic or regional outsoucing employment.

What factors cause domestic outsourcing and whether firm decisions about what to retain in-house and what to outsource have changes over time. Some evidence suggests that firms have responded by focusing on their core competencies and outsourcing low value added tasks as well as higher value added specialized functions. Advanced technologies have facilitated this process by allowing firms to outsource entire functions ans more easily monitor contractors as well as employees who work, leading to new forms of networked production and rise of specialized outsouring employment firms. Domestic outsoucing influences the changes of job quality, benefits, hours, workload, job stability, schedule stability and occupational safety, health, incidence of wage theft and access to training and promotions. Predictions are less clear for job requiring professional or technicial or specialized skills or those that are outsourced to large and diversified outsourced contractors. Types of outsourced contracts include: suppliers or vendors of products, such as manufacturing inputs or services, such as business services or staffs service or staffing firms, franchisees and independent contract, such as freelancers, independent contracts or non demand platform outsourced workers. It is significant restructuring of domestic manufacturing supply chains will greater reliance on suppliers and subcontractors. In addition, the potential growth of on demand outsourcing work as well as other forms of job fragmentation. It causes this question: How outsourced workers are multiple forms of income generating work to achieve economic security and how outsourcing workers can build career across jobs and over time.

Firm in every sector of the economy contract with other firms as part of their production process, as do governmental entities. The functions that are outsourced vary widely. For example: human resources ans research and development functions, building services, recycling, regulation and compliance, accounting, credit card collection, call centres, mortage and check processing, information technology and data processing, logistics and transportation, machine maintenance, cable installation, food services, food processing, parts manufacturing and assembly, laundry and housekeeping etc. outsourced jobs causes.

Whether what business impact of outsourcing will be caused? Nowadays, IT outsourcing was clearly a part of an effective management strategy that the companies felt IT outsourcing strategy can bring to achieve positive results. Information technology outsourcing providing servicers will be predicted to provide services that is expected to raise over the next five years minimum. The companies demand clients expected benefits of IT outsourcing and determined that cost reduction, increased operation, efficiency and improved IT effectiveness. What are the impacts of outsourcing to influence better long-term improvement in the business performance? It is impossible to being benefits of significant reduction and lower growth in sellings, general and administrative expense to IT outsourcing company demand clients. Also, pre-existing corporate cultures are focused on business improvement to IT outsourcing company demand clietns. In the past researches, some economists indicated that points can be used to reflect the actual numbers increase or decrease in percent. However, their prior researches shows that prior to outsourcing, the annual growth in selling, general and administration expenses of eompanies in the study was already 4.2 points lower than sector medium. Moreover, within one to two years after IT outsourcing these companies improved even most.

Annual growth in selling and general administrative expenses for them was 9.9 points lower efford to assist any IT outsourcing will have selling and administrative expenses for long term. Also, almost two-third of the companies studied outperformed in increased growth in return on asset two to three years after IT outsourcing commenced. Prior to outsourcing, the annual ROA growth rate for companies in the study ws 7.5 points lower than the sector median. After outsourcing, however these companies experienced 8.6 points higher median a substantial change of 16.1 points. Also, nearly two to third of the companies studied grew earnings faster than their peers. Two to three years after IT outsourcing, companies experienced an annual rate of growth in earnings 11.8 points higher than the growth rate of the sector median. Thus, it seems IT outsourcing can assist the IT outsourcing demand clients to reduce expenditure and to raise income both as the same time. Then, it will cause these questions to IT outsourcing demand clients. Is outsourcing influencing in an economic downturn to finance sector in the short term? Is the finance sector's renewed change for outsourcing just a temporary cost-cutting measure? Will today's economic climate initiate long term financial and productivity gains?

Whether what are benefits and disadvantages of outsourcing finance sector IT. I shall demonstrate why outsourcing open source software support and maintenance can be a good choice to start. Firstly when company plans to budget cuts expenditures, IT outsourcing is often the first choice. For example in 2003 year, Zurich Financial services' sprawling IT department consisted of more than 7,500 employees. After posting a record loss of 3.4 billion the year before, Zurich decided to cut down on in those staff and outsource nearly half of its IT work. Outsourcing has successfully cut costs by 45 percent and cut the number of in house IT staff by 60 percent. Here are some of the benefits that companies enjoy when they outsource information technology functions to competent, reliable vendors.

In fact, it can be too expensive to maintain, company's own information technology, especially during a recession. Fortunately, many IT functions can be easily and efficiently outsourced, positively impacting individual company's bottom line. Employee costs are much higher than just salary and benefits, keeping employees happy, productive and busy takes time, effort and money. Although, many IT staffs will be dismissed, it will increase the unemployment ratio in societies. But, moving an IT service out of house means financial organizations don't have to worry about technology refresh costs in the future. It also cuts down on human resources requirements, specialist IT service provides which can provide the newest technologies and deliver quality service more than company itself in house information provides are the most effective to develop and implement and upgrade their clients' software or the launch on a new platform, due to the expert's time is wasted on day-to-day duties for whose other IT outsourcing demand clients. However, instead of IT outsourcing service outsourced offshoring in that service sector, how economic impact to influence the outsourced offshoring country. For example, United States continues to run an international trade surplus in services. Many Americans are particularly concerned about the loss of skilled, well paid jobs in such fields as computer programming and accounting etc. positions. These jobs seemed relatively secure at a time when many manufacturing jobs were being cost to import competition. Similarly, telephone call centers, once viewed as an esonomic development opportunity in some areas, increasingly are moving low wage countries, such as India and the Philippines. Thus, offshoring raises many questions for policymakers and general public. For example, which service jobs will be affected most by import competition. What are the likely effects of service-sector offshoring on U.S.A. output, employment and our standard of living, such as America? Is offshoring really a problem that requires restrictive government actions or are other kinds of policies more appropriate to give Americans or other countries the highest possible living standard?

The term of offshoring refers to the relocation of jobs and production to a foreign country. The relocated jobs and production could be at a foreign office of the same multinational company or at a separate company located abroad. In constrast, the term outsourcing doesn't necessary imply that jobs and production are relocated to another country. The major outsourcing service jobs include human resource, accounting and information technology etc. in-house service jobs in large organizations. However, the loss of service jobs and factory production is caused by offshoring is diffuclt to measure. It is also difficult to determine the impact of offshoring on total services employment in the United States or other countries. International trade in services covers a wide range of industries and activites. For example, travel and transportation includes travel expenditures, passenger fares and frieght and port services, royalties and license fees cover transactions including patents, copyrights, trademarks and other intangible proprietary rights to use, produce or distribute products.

Other private services include many of these industries, such as education, financial services insurance, telecommunications and other professional services etc. Some economists indicated that occupational employment statistics for the Unisted States provided additional evidence that past service sector offshoring had been small. About 14 million service jobs were at risk of offshoring in 2000 year, when about 96 million service jobs had a low risk of ofshoring. The decline in the at-risk service occupations from 2000 year to 2002 year was about 218,000 jobs or roughly 109,000 jobs annually, relatively small number that is consistent with the estimates of McCarthy or Zandi.

In percentage terms, employment in the at risk occupations fell at a faster rate from 2000 year to 2002 year than in the low risk occupations. This faster decline is consistent with offshoring activity, although the decline is consistent with other explanations as well, such as faster of technological change in industries employing the risk occupations or greater cyclical sensitivity in these industries. Because offshoring was not the only cause of job loss in the risk occupations, the number of jobs moved offshore was undoubtedly less than 109,000 jobs annually. However, the estimates may understate the total impact because domestic companies with expanding worldwide employment may have located may of their newly created jobs abroad even when they didn't reduce their US employment. Some of those foreign jobs might provide services to US customers and potentially foreign jobs might provide service to US . Conversely, the estimates may overstate the total job loss from offshoring of the foreign outsourcing of some support jobs prevents the loss of other domestic jobs by keeping US firms competitive in world markets. For example, cost reductions from offshoring IT jobs might help a US financial services company win foreign contracts, preserving many professionals and support jobs in the US.

Lower production costs in foreign countries are a major cause of service sector offering. Although, the costs of land and other resources may be cheaper abroad, but the main difference betweeb the US and developing countries is labor costs. There is a large gap in computer programmer wages between the US and other countries. Any organizational capital includes both physical capital, such as machinery and computers and human capital , such as skills and knowledge. The cost savings is come from offshoring also might be reduced if the firm needed to pay higher transportation and telecommunication costs or management spends more time on service quality and data security. Still, the much lower levels of wages ans benefits in developing countries suggests that many services can be produced abroad at lower cost. The in-house professional relocation of labor-intensive service activities, such as legal transcription services to countries with lower labor costs is consistent with economists' basic theory of international trade, comparative advantage. So, in-house outsourced professional service will be a corporative advantage, if the country's legal profession is poor level to compare with the another country. e.g. the skill in-house the legal professional labors of the developing country, such as China is poor educational level to compare with the developed country, such as US. So, if China large organizations chose to outsource themselves in-house legal service jobs to outsource offshoring to US legal professional lawyers to do. It can bring comparative advantage to China large outsourced in-house legal service organizations, due to these China outsourced large organizations can reduce to employ to pay too much salaries to these many in-house Chinese domestic lawyers and the US outsourced legal consultants whose can give more professional legal recommendation to serve to the China large organizations.

In conclusion, although offshoring strategy can increase unemployment chance for this disadvantge. But, all of outsourcing benefits weighs are more than the offsourcing disadvantages. However, outsourcing strategy can have these benefits to the outsourced service demanders. Such as outsourcing is no longer just about cost saving, it is also a strategic tool that may power the twenty first century global economy. Moreover, outsourcing can increase productivity and competitiveness, e.g. for every 1000 jobs British Airways sends to India , the airline saves $23 million, companies can devote a portion of their outsourcing savings to helping employees make job transitions, also leader can no longer afford to view outsourcing as a business tactic, it is now essential to remain competitive. On the world stage, workers now compete globally, so individuals must continually learn more to vie successfully with their peers worldwide, the average company only spends about 20% of the value of its outsourcing contracts to manage its relationship with the outsource provider. So, in the positive view point, outsourcing strategy can bring a potential primary driver of the global economy development. Although, outsourcing can also cause the raising of domestic unemployment chance. But companies may soon be more outsourced than in sourced, signifying a fundamental reorganization that will affect employees, managers, customers and executives. Customers' choice will increase product costs will drop and workers' roles will change. Finally, the most important, the developing country will earn comparative advantage from the developed country's employers' offshoring jobs provision. Thus, the developing country's unemployment rate will be reduced, then the global economy will be kept more balance fairly.

Reference

Abrahamson, E., & Rosenkopf., (1993). Institutional and competitive bandwagons: Using mathematical modeling and a tool to explore innovation diffusion. Academy of management review, 18(3), 487-517.

Hill, C.W.L. & Jones, G.R. 1995. Strategic management, An integrated approach. Boston: Houghtom Mif In.

CHAPTER TWO

INFLUENCING ORGANIZATION OUTSOURCING STRATEGIES CHOICE FACTORS

Economy and management factors
   Economic factors influence
to meet strategic management?

What economic factors will influence any organizations to achieve their strategic plans successfully? Why does one firm cut prices when another firm buys out competitors? Why does one firm diversify into new industries, when another firm spins off subsidiaries to focus on its core ? Why do some strategic rise when others all? These organizations' activities will be influenced to choose to implement by economic factor influences.

These are central concern of both strategic management theorists and strategic management draw on diverse ideas as well as which have relationship to be influenced by unpredictable economic factors . So, organizations need to concern what external environment economic situation is. Such as development or decline (recession), then to decide how to adopt the most effective strategic plan to achieve the aim of effectiveness and efficiency more successfully. So, it seems that external economic environment factors can influence why organizations need an efficient and effective strategic plan to do more better.

Firstly, In organizational internal need hand , strategic management theorists need to view whose firm from different standpoints. Each strategist explores efficiency from the perspective of whose firm, developing theories of why one strategy is more successful then another, given product, service and industry characteristics.

Sociologists focus on efficiency from the perspective of the corporate environment itself, who neglect the exernal economic environment factor can influence the organization leaders how to implement their strategic plans. Developing theories about the context in which one strategy becomes defined as efficiency an effectiveness.

Secondly, In economic factor influences organizational strategic plan hand. Strategic management theorists need to begin with very different methodological imperatives. Strategists seek to develop adequate theories of why certain strategies are optional or at least efficient, based typically on insights from successful firms. Sociologists seek to explain variance in behavior across large populations of firms and over time, to research why potential causes for any economic situation.

These differences derive in part from their different goals, strategic management is oriented to develop concepts for cooperate leaders, whereas, economic sociology is oriented to explain the trends why to cause corporate behavior. For example, why does IKEA furniture business need to let any visitors who attempt to sit down to have comfortable feeling? Why does Apple brand computer business need to design and innovate any new model of notebooks and mobile computers.

In external economic environment influence, strategic theorists presume that firm behavior is driven principally by competitive pressure and quest for effectiveness and efficiency. Analysts tend to give great power to market factors and little power to historical, political and social factors. So, organization leaders need to concern how competitive pressures may lead whose firms to alter whose strategies, but the new strategies who choose are shaped by public policy, limitation, power and historical happen.

I shall indicate this question concerns why organizations need strategy plans. Why do firms diversify? In another view point to ask this question. Why is it efficient for some firms to diversify, and for which firms to diversify and for which firms is efficient and effective? Why do firms choose diversification? Why does a particular firm choose at a particular time? Economic sociologists usually ask this management challenges, who find organization challenges to give solution in economic view point. But for strategic management theorists, this problem concerns an argument based in efficiency. Question is such as: Can organizations make diversification efficient if which lack one efficent and effective strategy plan?

For economic sociologists, this problem is to explain the social processes behind the rise of a new business practice. Does it ensure to need diversification tend if the organization lacks an efficient and effective strategic plan to evaluate ? It's possible that diversification strategy can let multi-product firms are more profitable to campaign single product firms.

In the past, the diversification trend is during the 1980 year. What does cause this? On economic first view point, Davis et al. (1991) cite the inefficiencies inherent in diversification. Can strategy plan cause efficiency effect? On economic second view point , Davis also showed most firms make a mix of good and bad decisions, such that a disastrous strategy in product, which may be altered by a good one in marketing, or in human resources. On economic third view point, he also indicated firms seek to copy their profitable pears may have difficulty figuring out what to copy and may have difficulty copying it. However, sociologists certainly see managers as striving for efficiency . But managerial decisions , which are focus on how sociological processes to led managers to choose from an alternatives.

How to feel strategic thinking? Strategy took on a military significance and represented the action of commanding or leading armies in times of war, i.e. a military campaign. It meant a way of prevailing over the adversary, a tool of victory in war and why was it applied to other contexts and fields of human relationships: Political, economics, business, among others.

Into a field of knowledge in management, strategic management, with content, concepts and practice reasoning can be applied to any businesses. Management uses this old military concept to associate the activities of an organization's manager. Since it represents an important tools for business management in a competitive marketplace. The main objective of strategy involves preparing the organization to deploy the skills qualifications and internal resources of the enterprise.

So, it seems that strategic plan is similar to military campaign. If one country's soldier team lacks one efficient and effective military strategic plan to prepare to war, it is possible that the soldier team will fail, due to the soldier team lack one team leaders who can lead them how to organize whose team to co-operate efficiently. So, one organization will be failure to compete its competitors if which lacks one efficient strategic plan to prepare to organize which teams to co-operate to work from top level to middle level and down level in its organizational structure.

According to Obembe (2010) indicated knowledge management in an organization is begun by identifying the knowledge that individuals bring in from outside the company. In this case, the development of organizational strategy depends on understanding the perceptions of their managers on what strategy and strategic management actually is. The identification of perceptions of future managers on the concept is used in contributing significantly to organizational management practice. This enables the organizational knowledge on the field of strategy can hardly be managed should each manager understand the concept differently. So, if organization can have one efficient strategic plan, then it will raise ability to learn knowledge management skill to solve any human resource, strategic management etc. challenges more easily.

For example, Walt Disney entertainment theme park, which had innovated one efficient knowledge management strategy to reduce visitors' complains and dissatisfaction, such as designing fast ticket queue system, which can reduce visitors' queue time. Although, admission fee is more expensive to compare to normal ticket buyers. But who can choose not to need to wait long time to queue to play more than one kind entertainment facility to play. If who can come back the prior entertainment facility queue within one hour, who do not need to queue again to play the prior entertainment facility. So, who can reduce queue time to chose to play any prior queue entertainment facilities within one hour coming back, who will feel more satisfactory to spend loss queue working time to play different entertainment facilities. Also, when any visitors feel need to enquire how to go to anywhere , who can find cleaners to enquire how to go anywhere conveniently and easily. Because the cleaners will give map to indicate any location to let who to know. So, any visitors do not need to spend much to find to any visible map noticeboard to find location. Cleaners can tell to them how to go to any anywhere to let them know more clearly. So, knowledge management is one kind of strategic thinking to solve customer individual psychological dissatisfactory feeling. The Disney leaders need to continue to discover to seek any weakness points to solve customer psychological satisfactory feeling or need from daily observation in Disney entertainment park.

Strategy is a business logic, rational and sequential to the most dynamic that understand this process as associated with culture and learning factors, political and power relations. Thus, there are two major problems affecting the understanding of what the concept of strategy really means that confusion is between strategy and effectiveness tools as well as confusion is between strategy and strategic planning. The rook of the problem seems to be the lack of a full understanding as to what strategy really is.

Organizational strategy can mean different in scale and complexity, which can mean policies, objectives, tactics, goals, programs, among others. However, the concept of strategy has been used indiscriminately in the field of management, meaning anything from a precisely formulated course of action, a positioning in a particular environment, through to the entire personality and existential rational behind a company's existence. Strategy is not only one way of dealing in a competitive environment or market, as treated by much of the literature and its popular use, as it can't only summarize the ideas, proposals, guidelines. This fact has an explanation. Strategy in organizations , as a field of study is much newer than its current practice, and its knowledge remains under construction.

Some strategic professionals think strategy is such as: what matters are for the effectiveness of the organization, the external point of view, which stresses the relevance of the objectives against the environment, in terms of internal stresses, balanced communication between members of the organization and a willingness to contribute towards actions and the achievement of common objectives, analyzing the present situation and changing at whenever necessary to find what one's resources are or what which should be.

It is the determinant of the basic long-term goals of a firm and the allocation of resources necessary for carrying out these goals, it is a rule for making decision to be determined by product/market scope growth, competitive advantage and synergy. So, it is a thinking to any leaders to be prepared to make any decisions and develops the learning process in organization as well as it is the pattern of objectives, purposes or goals and major policies and plans to achieve missions for any organization within a limited time prediction or expectation.

All business organizations are concerned with low which will survive and prosper in the future. A business strategy is often thought of as a plan or set of intentions that will set the long term direction of the actions. However, how organizational plans or how intent , an organization's strategy can only become a meaning reality to achieve include corporate, business and function three levels.

The top corporate level key issues concern that what businesses shall be in , acquire or divest, how allocate resources what the relationship businesses and center is . The middle business level key issues concern that how businesses compete, what the mission is, what the strategic objectives are. The low function level key issues concern that how the function contribute to the business strategy, what the strategic objectives are managed in the function, what technology is used in the function, what skills are required by workers in the function.

Organizations need to concern these questions. Is the strategy consistent between the organization's strategy and business strategy, between operation strategy and the other functional strategy, between the different decision areas of operation strategy? Does the strategy contribute to competitive advantage? Enabling operations to set priorities that enhance competitive advantage, high opportunities for operations to complement the business strategies, making operations strategy clear to the rest of the organization, providing the operating capabilities that will be required in the future.

Organizations need have operations performance objectives to measure which performance. It is a criterion against which to evaluate the performance of operations. There are considered to be five possible operations performance objectives, cost , quality, speed, dependability and flexibility. Such as, the ability to produce at low cost, the ability to produce with specification and without error, the ability to do things quality in response to customer demands and offer short lead times between a client orders and a product or service and when who receive it, the ability to deliver products and services with promises made to clients, e.g. in a quotation or other published information, the ability to change operations. Flexibility includes the ability to change the volume of production, to change the time taken to product, to change the mix of different products or services produced , to innovate and introduce new products and services. Thus, these are basic organization structure of strategic management.

How to apply strategic planning and management in public and private sector organizations and what are their differences?

Management issues can be divided in two groups: governmental or public, with its specific aims, methods and challenges, and private sector responsible for economical results, competitiveness and state revenues. How can strategic planning, management and leadership of public and private sectors identify opportunities to improve performance with differences? Concerning this research, some strategic management professional had attempted to do research to conclude that in public sector there is great emphasis on strategic planning part of management process, but implementing plan to clear activities delays or is even misled. In private sector enterprises tend to look short term. Otherwise, thus gaining results in small every day actions , but looking greater sight to future and therefore to get chance of greater growth . Government should implement more client-oriented approach using best example from entrepreneurial world. Private sector should learn how to generate concrete long term plans, delegate duties and not to mix responsibilities in enterprise for greater result. So , who concluded that strategic plan is considered that private sector prevails over the public sector in efficiency and result oriented actions. Although, this assumption reasoned with lots of practical examples and arguments and efficiency's prevalence of private sector over the public administration was proved.

Considering the public administration strategic plan, the strategic management professionals argument do not encourage public administration to work in its own self-interest, but who discovered more efficient environment where to find the best management practices, in stance in field of customer care, that can be adopted in a legal and rational way.

Public sector is advocated that intellectual work is more hierarchical , within the team work more knowledgeable team member for a special task will already to be an informal interim leader, regardless of the structure of hierarchy, to compare to private sector hierarchical structure. They showed that are subordinated hierarchically to the long term development planning documents. The short term development planning documents are subordinated hierarchically to the median term developed planning documents. According to the updated system all public administration situation should develop the action strategy from the period of three years that serves for the budget planning and allocation to compare to provide sector. Otherwise, strategic planning in private enterprises come within strategic management and contributes as part of it. Strategic management is focused defining of business mission, the company's development direction, objectives and the resources and long-term management decision -making for implementing the strategy .

Why is middle management important in strategic organizational chart structure? Middle level managers, their role no longer entails issuing orders to subordinates. In fact, middle level managers in flat organizations may have very few direct reports. The most successful middle managers must rely on strong influencing skills and the ability to a complex network of resources critical role in the ultimate ability of a company to achieve its strategic goals. For example, marketing managers and engineering directors, there are the middle level managers who are being asked to do more with fewer resources. They are being held responsible have no direct organizational authority. They are being asked to influence partners, drive into unfamiliar channels, and motivate complex networks of global resources to get results .

So, employers or top managers, leaders need to concern whether who have worked relative pressure from worked relative causes. And yet ongoing restructuring, the dissolution of the career ladder, and persistent job insecurity have eroded middle level managers' sense at loyalty, frequently leaving them feeling demoralized and disenfranchised. Because it has chance, these middle level managers who are at risk of leaving your organization, unless you provide the proper support and development to perform their new responsibilities. Higher turnover among this crucial middle manager group , risks undermining company performance and diminishing the vital connection between strategy and execution. With more pressure , greater responsibilities , less training and fewer resources at the command. IS it any wonder that many middle level managers are suffering from increasing levels of stress?

Companies recognize that such high turnover rates will significantly to implement to middle level management to hope them to achieve strategic objectives. So, it seems , instead of top and low levels management, middle level management ought to be the most important role in any organizations. Because these middle level managers are such as middle communication staffs , who need to listen top level management to let the top level managements to know how to do whose job duties in most efficient methods and effective final results to achieve organization's expectation. So, any strategic plan implement must need whose assistance to finish plan more easily.

Management factors influence organizational strategic plans
Nowadays, many countries public institutions had implemented total quality management. For example, in the United States, strategic planning

was introduced after the 1900 year with much of the early literature focusing on local government applications (Poister and Streib, 2005;45). The emphasis in strategic management approaches to be more in focused on a future time horizon. Ideally, strategic management attempts to achieve future goals by liking strategic initiatives to operational process. When total quality management is also forced looking and seeks long-range improvements, applications also emphasize attention to current quality and citizen satisfaction concerns.

So, strategy means the determination of the basic long-term goals and objectives of an enterprise, and the adoption of actions and the allocation of resources how to carrying and these goals. It is the pattern of decisions in a company that determines and reveals its objectives, purposes or goals, produces the principal policies and plant for achieving those goals, and defines the range of business, the company is to purpose, the kind of economic and human organization , it is or intends to be , and the nature of the economic and non-economic contribution , it intends to make to its shareholders, employees, customers and societies.

Is strategy implementation suitable to apply the public sector? It depends on whether perceived service is affective, efficient and equity to department departments. A logical incremental and mostly rational style of implementation are associated with better effectiveness, efficiency and equity, with the absence of an implementation style associated with worse performance.

Nowadays, strategy management tools and ideas been brought into play by governments across the world to enhance capacities and performance standards in the force of in face of increasingly challenging. In response, researchers have begun to investigate whether management can be applied to strategic public organizations. What are the relationship between different strategy implementation styles and the effectiveness and efficiency? Is a rational strategy implementation styles associated with good organizational performance? Does an incremental strategy implementation style have a stronger or weaker relationship with performance or weaker relationship with performance than a rational one? Does some combination of the two styles result in the best performance outcomes? What is relationship between strategy implementation styles and the perceived effectiveness, efficiency and equity to public sector?

To answer above questions. It is important to know that the actual content of those strategies and the way in which were initially formulated to public sector if any public organizational departments want staffs work efficient and effective and equity. The introduction of new public service delivery models, monitoring the effectiveness of how public departments operational evaluation system and culture requires to fit a distinction between more or less planned styles of implementation tends to be top-down and hierarchical, involving the use of prepared action plans, performance monitoring, and review processes to any government departments.

In theory, private and public organizations may adopt different implementation styles for different purpose, for example, using a highly formal process for introducing an efficiency, focused strategy, when adopting an incremental approach to the explanatory search for innovative solutions to service delivery problems to public needs for any public sector departments. An emphasis on a rational implementation style is thought to result in better public sector and department organizational performance because the goal clarity on which it facilities the on-going inter-department coordination of internal and external activities between public sector's different departments.

Overall, the evidence from the private sector suggests that a rational strategy implementation style is associated with better organizational performance. However, decisions from private and public organizations are found that strategic planning has a stronger positive influence on the success of implementation than a more ad-hoc approach in which decisions are made on an incremental basis as situations. For example, Hickson et al (2003) study exploring implementation style and performance in a sample of public and private organizations finds that a dual approach combination elements of both planned and adoptive implementation has a stronger positive association with organizational performance than an emphasis on either planning or adaptation. Thus, it beings this hypothesis, such as a logical incremental strategy implementation style will have a stronger positive relationship with organizational performance then either a rational or incremental implementation style.

Due to public organization is a hierarchical structure. I suggest that a logical incremental and a mostly rational implementation style are associated with higher levels of effectiveness, efficiency and equity than other implementation styles, with no clear approach associated with the lowest level of performance to any public departments. Strategic decision theory is an important school of thought in management studies. So, policy markers need to seek how to improve the effectiveness, efficiency, effectiveness and equity of local public services should therefore consider the extent to which it is possible to encourage incremental adaption of strategies.

Organization strategic plan challenges

School strategic plan challenges

In researching this question how to achieve the greatest level of effectiveness to school organizations. This can be measured through a conceptualization process of the S.W.O.T. (strengths, weaknesses, opportunities, threats) environmental analysis, clearly defined mission statement, goals and objectives, specific strategy formulation outline, implementation of the strategies and control of the strategic plan. This conceptualization control process is the action that will link the independent variable of efficient strategic plans, through the original measurements of the steps of those plans.

Why do school organizations need an efficient strategic plan? School strategic plan is thinking and responding satisfy social education to adopt student and school cultural, and to adopt economic influence threat factors. Strategic planning is needed at the point when priorities begin to compete with another one school. It is necessary to have specific goals for any activities or decision to measure school effectiveness in addition to thinking strategically for long term education success.

There are many different dimensions to school planning classified according to :(i) the time involvement of the school plan, (ii) the school organizational level performing the plan, e.g. classroom control performing, teaching performance etc. (iii) the activities involved in the school plans, e.g. what is the standard (criteria) to decide school fee charge amount, each course of student maximum numbers per year, how to design each course content and (iv) the general characteristics of purpose of the school plans , e.g. mission, education development long term plan.

The criteria of school effectiveness include such as, significant relational student groups to foster a sense of close relationship between teachers and students, providing opportunities of each student group for learning sharing, each student personal psychological caring and belonging, strong teaching leadership resources that are characterized by the presence of a key teaching groups of strong experienced teaching leaders, that compliment the leading the lack experiences teachers, and who how a set of strategic educational objectives outlining what who are to accomplish each course teaching structure, participatory decision-making, characterized by ownership and openness to diverse beliefs and opinions between experienced teachers and lack experienced teachers, classroom space and teaching facilities that will provide flexibility as well as classroom to growth and expansion for the needs (demands) of student numbers increasing.

So, it seems an effective school strategic plan is broad in scope and identifies how a school organization will commit its resources over a pre-selected period. It is a long term plan analyzing and creating objectives to reach a specific set of education goals. When the school strategic plan is incorporated, it involves dividing and assigning the responsibilities of each education task with specified resources and completion target dates. The advantages of planning help schools adapt to changing education environments and specifies to whom the responsibilities belong. It gives a sense of direction for assessing the education market position and establishing education objectives, priorities and strategies to accomplish the education goals with motivation.

For educational strategic planning has these basic steps processes including: the external educational environment analysis internal and external analysis, a clearly defined education mission statement with educational goals and objectives, education formulation and implementation and control. The first stage of development, an education strategic plan is an analysis of the external educational environmental opportunities and threats of an educational organization, (strengths, weaknesses, opportunities, threats) analysis. This external overview includes analysis of the macro environmental forces, educational industry environment and trends. Macro environmental forces including: the political and legal , economic , technological and social forces. For example, school organizations can evaluate which countries economic situation to predict student family financial afford, if the country unemployment ratio is high, it is possible that students need more student loans in the year, if the country technological production industry 's need is much, then it is possible that engineering , computer subjects demand will increase, if the country's political and legal system is stable, it is possible that the low and policy subjects demand will increase. So, schools need to concern whether what external environment is occurring to predict what kinds of demands (needs) of including a schools' resources, mission statement and goals. It also entails the sustained competitive advantage, which is the structure of human (staffs), e.g. teachers, clerks, computer technicians etc. as well as school organizational and physical resources, e.g. classroom facilities, school library, classrooms and offices furniture and computer facilities etc. The mission statement is the reason for the existence of the organization. Such as school organization mission statement can be providing professional knowledge to prepare students career development, providing reasonable school fees to educate poor students. To be the top university at school world rank, providing high educational quality service to let students to study in an enjoyable environment. Following, schools need to know or plan what which short term plan educational goals and objectives are. For example, goals and objectives will be increased double student number in the end of this year or will be increased double school fee income more than 30% each course and it has no influence to reduce student current enrolling number in the end of year. For long term plan example, goals and objectives will be raised famous and loyal university rank within the 100 rank from world university rank between five and ten years. Finally, the most important reason why any school needs an effective strategic plan. Any school can revise what challenges which will encounter and which can find the reasons why which can not achieve to implement whose original educational goals and objectives and to attempt to find the methods to solve these challenges to achieve which objectives and goals more easily. Even, if the school ensures to achieve its goals and objectives. Strategic plan can let which to find what needs to be improved to adopt to satisfy which potential student needs. Thus, an effective strategic plan can let any school to achieve its objectives and goals more easier as well as to revise and either to find reasons why which can not achieve which objectives and goals or to measure what which needs to do to improve its strategic plan more effective when the school has achieve its objectives and goals ensure. Thus, it seems the school can achieve its objectives and goals more easier in a effective and logic attitude if the school can have an effective strategic plan to predict what challenges it will encounter during its strategic plan achievement process.

Service organizationsveffectiveness
and efficiency challenges
The service concept plays role in service design and new service development in service or manufacturing industry. The service concept indicates the how and the what of service design and helps mediate between customer needs and an organization's strategic intent.
A service organization can only delivers a service after outsourcing investments in numerous assets, processes, people and materials. Much

like manufacturing a product composed of components, services similarly consist of components. However, unlike a product, service components are often not physical entitles, but rather are a combination of processes, people skills and materials that must be appropriately planned or designed service. In designing a new service of redesigning can existing service, service managers must make decisions about each component of the service, from major decisions like facility location to seemingly minor decisions like supervising workers. For even a relatively simple service, numerous decisions are made in taking a new or redesigning service from the idea stage.

In many cases, these processes are ongoing as service organization continue to invest in their physical assets , these processes are of their workforce as well as make changes and improvements. The strategic level to the operational and service encounter levels. A major challenge for service organization is ensuring that decisions each of these levels are made consistently, focused on delivering the reasonable or satisfactory service performance to targeted customers. Any services include physical and non-physical components both. Or do customers need a service as a singular outcome who are seeking when who obtain or purchase the service? e.g. restaurant waiter service, cinema ticket sale service and cinema seat seeking helper etc. Similarly how do service providers (i.e. service employee) provide excellent service attitude to satisfy customer expectation successful, such as one satisfy customer expectation successful, such as one package of restaurant or cinema watching movie of service. Customers have a preconceived notion of what a service is, even who have not experienced it previously (Johnston and Clack, 2001). So, service providers need to provide excellent service performance or attitude to satisfy any customers' real preconceived psychological needs if who hope customers must choose to consume whose service again, e.g. restaurant or cinema service etc. any shopping service consumption choices.

Before, during and after service delivery, service organizations need to arrange excellent service to satisfy consumer's needs or expectations. These expectations relate to the nature of the nature of the service package, as well as to the nature of service, during the service encounters. So, to ensure the service package and service encounter to satisfy the customer's needs and service organization, itself must focus on the design and delivery of whose service concept.

Some psychologists indicate service concept has three levels. First, the service concept is how it drives design decisions for new and redesigned services. An organization's definition of its service concept is necessary at the strategic level of planning. Second, who describe how the service concept is useful at the operational level during service concept is useful at the operational level during service design planning, particularly in service strategy into the service delivery system and in determining appropriate performance measures for evaluating service design. Third, who indicate service recovery, one component of service design it used to show the usefulness of applying the service concept in designing and enhancing service encounter interactions. They propose that it is critical to clearly define the service concept before and during the design and development of services. The service concept then serves as a driver of the many decisions made during the design of service delivery systems and service encounters. Johnston and Clark (2001) further defined the service concept as: service operation is the way in which the service is delivered; service experience is the customer's direct experience of the service; service outcome is the benefits and results of the service for the customer ; and the value of the service is the benefits to the customer perceives as inherent in the service weighed against the cost of the service. So, service concept includes operation, experience, outcome and value four aspects. The service concept is not only defined the how and the what of service design, but also ensures integration between the low and the what. Furthermore, the service concept can also help mediate between customer needs and the organization's strategic intent. One reason for poorly perceived service is the mismatch between what the organization intends to provide (its strategic intent) and what its customers may require to expect (customer needs).

Without a clear and shared understanding of the nature of service to be provided, i.e. the service concept, how can an service manager expect to design a successful service? For example, a car salesperson needs to explain the characteristics and quality and speed and safety issues to let the customer to understand what the functions are for the car. The car salesperson needs to know how to give the excellent customer feedback service to persuade the customer to choose to buy the car easily. So, the role of car salesperson (service provider) who needs to know what the car manufacturing technology, car engines physical facilities and equipment to prepare to give enough information of the car to let the customer to know. Then, the chance of successful sale will be increased.

In conclude, service concept includes these steps: The first step is service strategy, which includes inputs elements, such as staffs, technology, processes, physical facilities and equipment. Next step is service delivery system, which indicates how staffs perform whose service. The, the step is outputs, which include service outcomes and service experience. Finally, the step is performance, whether the performance is efficient and effective as well as how the service provider will measure and will give feedback to its performance. So, service concept is one system process and it is a cycle process.

Electronic health record system
to health care organization challanges

Why strategic management concept (planning) is needed to apply to any hospital organizations , when which needs to apply electronic health record system to serve client records for administration. Nowadays, these factors have been facilities to new model of health care delivery to hospitals, such as electronic health record (EHR) system. Electronic health records care professionals, health care systems and governments. The use of EHR is growing rapidly in various countries including the UK, the USA, and Australia. Each country has developed its own methods of design, adoption and implementation. However, they face many challenges, particularly relating to interoperability, privacy and security. Thus, health care organizations need have good strategic plan to meet the electronic health record system chance needs to satisfy customer needs for excellent health care service. The strategic plan includes how to describe the definition and features of primary health care service, such as what is the health care service, such as what is the health care organization's core value(s), principle(s), objective(s), and elements of a primary health care system, how to arrange the primary health care team and how to give the benefits and how to solve the challenges of primary health care teams in the health care service organization.

Healthcare is influenced by a range of factors, like new technology, advances in medicine and society expectations. A healthcare delivery system is a way of organizing health services. It is finite resources. So, as patient's expectations grow, it has to be managed effectively and efficiently by government throughout the world. Primarily, healthcare is delivered through primary care centers, which deal with patients whose healthcare can be managed outside of the hospital. Secondary, healthcare is managed in hospital. Tertiary care providers more sophisticated care in specialist medical centers. So, health care strategic plan is needed to designed to follow who will manage it, such as government or hospital or medical centers. For example, to develop the electronic health record system, each health care service organization needs to concern how to apply the electronic health record system to provide the most fast speedy, the most safe and the most excellent quality care to serve patients satisfactory. Health was once defined and thought to be influenced by people's habit relating to lifestyle, exercise, the environment and food (Stanhope & Lancaster, 2000). Later, health was seen only as the freedom from disease (physical or mental). So, patient service is related to physical or mental needs in any health care service organizations usually.

In the future, because electronic health record (EHR) system will be popular to be used to serve patients for any health care service organization, such as clinics, hospitals, medical centers, psychological illness health care clinics etc. It is therefore suggested that political leaders at the Ministry of health need to establish a broad vision for how EHR will be developed in the future. This vision must be influenced by all the main stakeholders. By consulting with these stakeholders and thus involving them in defining the EHRs, it development and maintenance of the EHRs. To ensure that the adoption process runs smooths and never loses direction. It is proposed that government staff should prepare a strategic roadmap, which will enable resources and actions to be prioritized to ensure effectiveness and efficiency. The strategic plan " tool" has become increasingly important in dealing with the continually changing environment of the health care setting. So, it is well placed to monitor the health system for any potential threats or challenges from encountering patients' needs immediately in any hospitals, clinics or medical centers. So, the strategic plan can also be used to coordinate stakeholder involvement, monitor and utilize policy changes, coordinate the involvement of potential users in the design and implementation of potential users in the design and implementation of the electronic health record system, assess and priorities finances and coordinate human resources. So, this health electronic record system will be a popular tool to sustain direction and action for any health care service organization in the future. Hence, any health care service organization need to use electronic health care system to adopt to the new change needs for patient service. As the same time, any health care service organizations' strategic plan ought to follow how to design its health care system to implement its strategic plan, then those health care service organizations will be more easy to achieve whose objectives or goals or missions. So, it means that how to design the health care service organization's electronic health record system. Then, it will know how to implement its strategic plan more easy.

Benefits of rationalization from
strategic plans
    Reducing costs and improving
service for strategic plan to service organizations
In general, organizations throughout the public and
private sectors face to improve support for operations, reduce costs, and improve efficiency. In most, organizations, the costs for operating and managing applications makes up from 75 % to 80% percent of the budget. The emphasis on ongoing portfolio governance, system that cost reduction strategic plan for operational plans to any departments.
Application rationalization means : selecting organizational application based on business and prioritizing related actions (choosing what the business will to and what which won't do), effectively managing the value of both existing and proposed applications, monitoring changing priorities and application value in real time, continually reviewing and adjusting as necessary, application inventory is the process of rationalizing the business applications begins with capturing in inventory of all applications currently in use.
One element that characterizes these efforts is that which one usually one-time events marked by a statistic method to collect application data, which results in a new statistic information that is probably different from and unrelated to the one collected 18 months earlier. Some painful meaning analysis is done on the collected data, and a few actions might be taken. The rationalization questions may include: How does the application fit with technical standards? Does staff have the necessary skills set to use it to best advantage? Are users satisfied with its performance and benefits? Are there better alternatives? What are the maintenance costs? Mergers and acquisitions, application rationalization can be performed before and after mergers and acquisitions to assess the best strategic fit. The value and impact to apply rationalization strategic plan method to reduce cost and improve service benefits for operational plans to any departments.
Business process management, application rationalization can provide insights into gaps or redundancies in the current application portfolio,

enhancing an application's ability to finish any business process more efficiently. In doing so, the business can introduce innovation products, provide customer service, and manager risk more efficiently and effectively compliance management. Organizations need to know of their application rationalization at its every department from an aggregate compliance score perspective, how to manager the application investment from a lifecycle management perspective.

By consolidation technical strategic plan, organizations are able to reduce the costs of different departments. They provides cost reduction to overall business expenditures which enables new products and technologies that drive the bottom line. For example, vendor price reduction management rationalization can apply efficient management for vendor negotiations by giving them the advantage of a detailed application, e.g. inventory numbers. The risks associated with it, and its business value. Once on an even playing field, the organization can negotiate wisely and put terms into on agreement that place demands back on the vendor to reduce risk or add business value, going way part pursuing price reductions. For another example, prior to outsourcing strategy , experts say organizations should have a good sense of the value of investments, which have already made, the value and risks of outsourcing and specifically what whose money is accomplishing through their outsourcing negotiation. Knowing what assets are in their application portfolio and what services which need to acquire will ensure that business set up the right outsourcing agreement. Next example, audit prioritization and remediation is critical to know which aspects of operations run the highest business and technical risk, so which can be articulated and addressed. An efficient audit solution allows executive to share insight into such risk by enabling them to create a single system of audit and record that gives consistent live view of the business benefits of their application , e.g. inventory numbers. Quantifying these benefits will be specific to the particular organization. For example, if one large insurance company could discover that 15% of its insurance applications could be decommissioned immediately with no impact to its insurance business, resulting in substantial savings. Then, insurance company will choose to spend 37% of its time on maintenance of insurance applications and 63% of its time on new project development, a complete reversal from how the organization divided its time three years ago. Thus, prediction what will occur to cause any business loss or cost increasing that can influence the business have more benefits to decide to spend more time to choose to do the more beneficial projects in order to reduce long term cost spending and raise long term benefits. So, behavioral rationalization can influence the business's correct time spending to which aspects of investment projects to earn more returns.

Brand strategy

Managers need to consider the customer and other stakeholder with their branding efforts to make appropriate making decisions because brands is such at the strategic organizational assets. Management at this valuable asset needs to strategic thinking and position. The fast innovation, increased service levels and diminishing brand loyalty characterizing today's marketplaces have led to corporate branding becoming a strategic marketing tool (Xie and Boggs, 2006).

A successful brand can be defined an identifiable product, service, person or place augmented in such a way that the buyer or user perceives relevant, unique added values which match their needs most closely. What kinds of product brand can influence consumer choice? For example, product like milk, tin, iron ore and potatoes , vegetables come to mind where purchase decisions tend to be taken on the basis of price or availability and not on the expensive products brand can influence consumer choice, e.g. cars , wash machines, televisions , air conditioners etc. manufacturing products.

Conceptually, branding appears to be a necessary means of building sales by identifying products and services. Branding is the initial means to build consumer awareness by naming the offer, but also by distinguishing the offer from other similar products or services within an established category. Branding is about being different (Kay, 2006).

When a company can create strong brand , it can attract customer preference and company is more protected against a company initiatives, and company can plan a growth through the penetration of new markets. So, if a business can have a strong brand, it can ensure a company's long-term success in possible. It can create goodwill value in consumption market to influence each consumer choice when who needs to buy the kind of manufacturing product. A brand combines physical and psychological element both. The physical aspect creates the linkage between differentiating them from other enterprises or products. The psychological aspect of a brand constitutes the maintenance of uniformity in terms of communications, guarantees ad behaviors as well as consistency and conformity to particular requirements (Chovancova, 2012).

Brand strategy refers to the ways that firms mix and match their brand's name on their products and a firms through its products, presents itself to the world. Corporate brand strategy must be developed to deliver the highest gains to all stakeholders and corporate public (Shahri, 2011). The brands as strategic assets and resources of competition advantages for organizations in changing and high competition world need to strategic attention and consideration from them. Strategic management organizational strengthens and weaknesses (internal factors) and environmental opportunities and threats (external factors) and environmental opportunities and threats (external factors). Also, strategic brand management can be viewed from these internal (identify) and external (image) perspective. So, establishment of balance is needed between the brand identity and image , e.g. LG brand mobile phones will be built different attractive mobile images, e.g. mobile phone products design of any model choices as well as correct identity attributes ,e.g. music sound choices attributes, internet attributes, phone call attributes by the LG brand mobile phone manufacturer. So, the suggested LG brand models can help multi-business companies operating and guideline to selection and choice of LG mobile phone branding strategy to enter the global competition mobile phone sale market, e.g. mobile phone mature market , e.g. Hong Kong, US, UK, mobile phone potential (developing market) , e.g. India, Africa.

It is evident that this LG brand different model mobile phone products can be chosen to enter to emerging or developing markets. It can be a proper guidance to individual (single) mobile phone business companies (from developed) economies entering to emerging or developing economies or companies operating in emerging markets. So, LG brand mobile phone can have the strength of relationship between influencing factors and choice of branding strategy is moderated by other situation-dependent influences if it chose to join to be another brand of mobile phone partner. Because of broader the stakeholders' interest, the LG non famous brand mobile phone firm can operate in emerging markets , e.g. US market more likely will phone corporate branding with any one famous brand mobile phone firm in US.

In emerging market, such as US mobile phone brand market, there are many different stakeholders that affect LG brand mobile phone organization enters to US mobile phone market. In this US mobile phone market , corporate image is emphasized by stakeholders more and more, therefore entrants from developed countries , such as US, is possible to choose corporate branding more likely. Developing economies experience political and legal instabilities daily, as a result, it can be suppose that corporate branding can manage these instabilities and decrease their effects. Because lack of valid and reliable information , media and other communication channels to Korea , LG brand mobile phone company, the marketing costs are very high in developing economies , such as Korea and companies prefer corporate branding strategy with US any one famous brand mobile phone company. So, such as one Korea, non famous LG brand mobile phone company which can choose to enter the developed country, such as US market to corporate with any one famous brand mobile phone company to build corporate brand strategy if which believed its LG brand mobile models have unique functions (attributes), when US any famous brand mobile phone companies' models of mobile phones have lack of these unique functions from LG brand mobile phone products.

Human resource plans to space
exploration organization
The European space exploration decides on investment in space science. I shall indicate how it is carrying on implementing strategic human resource plan presence in space mission to achieve its space exploration aim. Application-oriented space programs, such as telecommunications, navigation and Earth observation are fully served by robotic (i.e. fully automated) satellites. Where a strategic human resource presence plan would be demanded environmental requirement of these state-of-the art instruments. Yet the exploration of the nearby solar system , for example, the Moon and Mar mission may be conducted in principle by either robotic vehicles and/or a human presence. Hence, an excellent strategic human resource plan is really needed if European space exploration expected its space exploration mission can be success. To justify future space exploration, especially in the area where robotic and human spaceflight capabilities overlap. To provide guidance, we must examine some strategy aspects of this potentially powerful robot-human partnerships long-term strategic human partnership plan.
Scientific enquiry(including life and engineering sciences), broader consideration of technology and economy as well as more philosophical and political aspects. European space exploration must need different international scientists cooperation from different scientific professionals to cooperate to research different scientific skills to achieve space

exploration more easily. Because European space exploration mission is expected to earn economic and societal benefits of funding pure science and space science missions. Indeed, a strategic human resource plan for the cost share between robotic and manned missions in European space exploration, capitalizing on technological advance and international cooperation, but without negative impacting the future of pure scientific research, would be highly desirable. Hence international different scientists need to cooperate to achieve this space science exploration mission more easily. First European space exploration needs have clear strategic plan for human space flight missions. Such as: achieving scientific, political, and commercial activities dealing with the Earth, e.g. meteorology, climate , resources, communications, navigation, military and surveillance, achieving activities related to the exploration of the solar systems typically scientific , and which may be either robotic or manned. Thus, European policies and activities are needed reasonable well focused and organized of with the selections of missions in each of areas being determined by evolving scientific developments and commercial priorities, when European needs to cooperate with some space exploration countries, such as China, England, Japan, US, India etc. countries. For example, an objective and strategic consideration of some aspects of the future of solar system exploration might begin process with a significant impact on long-term European ambitions and policies.

European space exploration needs to consider how to develop a strategic view. The term space exploration represents to extension of human reach beyond the Earth's atmosphere using spacecraft to access unknown environments and to acquire knowledge about space planets, stars by human and robotic means.

From a purely scientific perspective, the exploration of the solar system mission is such as, understanding the formation of the solar system and of the Earth, and questions of plane more generally. It also addresses questions related to he beginning of life on Earth, and the search for evidence for (past) life and biological activity, elsewhere in the solar system and beyond.

From a human space flight perspective, space exploration mission represents the outward continuation of Earth based exploration, which has advanced over many centuries. These activities, ranging from the Apollo program, the current international space station activities, and future plans for manned missions to Mars have a strong impact on the public, at the same time, associated costs are very large.

From long term plan, from a economical benefit human space flight perspective, European space exploration organization objectives include: To raise students knowledge and learning to understand the solar system and of the universe as whole, to assist university to increase space science course (subjects school fee income and to encourage student numbers to choose to study this space exploration course (subjects as well as provides many different kinds of space exploration job chance for students space science employment market, for civilized and advanced society for universities education, employers capital investment and research to earn long term economic benefits to overall European economic development; space science research is as an extension of the pursuit of pure research , entirely unexpected and unpredictable economic development can eventually deliver substantial benefits to European society, and related economic dividend, more calculated approaches to exploiting potential arising from space research are being increasingly well coordinated.

Space technology transfer program (and its associated business incubations center), for example, has been set up to share the benefits of its research and development, making space sector technologies available to European industry, technology development has more immediately, space exploration provides new challenges, requiring the direct development of new technologies. These technological development can create new possibilities for innovation and economic growth , spanning business opportunities for industry as well as access to new resources. This provides the strong motivation both for politicians and tax payers to commit to their very high costs, space exploration encourages industrial development return is the strong industrial interest to develop large-scale facilities and capabilities for space exploration, space exploration has the capability of spectacularly demonstrating national and international capabilities, and has the potential of fostering international cooperation in ambitions projects of international human resource cooperation . At the same time, industrial countries and Europe as a whole, do not want to be left behind in the commercial aspects of space exploration, but rather want to be considered as viable collaborative partners by other space faring countries and organizations . For Europe, this means maintaining a level of space exploration know how such that other key players (USA, Japan, China, Russia, as well as emerging investors like India and Brazil) consider that it provides. Thus, European space exploration needs different countries scientists cooperation to achieve space business objectives, space research objectives, space education objections. It needs have human resources strategic plan to assist to any related space technological aspect research if European expected its space exploration mission can be achieves on one day. Thus, strategic human resource plan is very important to European space exploration organization.

For strategic human resource plan, I shall indicate these aspects as below:

In the area of human health, international space station (ISS) research is providing in the understanding of ageing, disease and the environment. Biological and human investigations have provided an improved understanding of basis physiological processes normally masked by gravity and the development of new medical technology driven by the need to support telemedicine, disease models, psychological stress response systems, nutrition, cell behavior and environmental health . So, human strategic plan needs this medical, biological, environmental health, psychological health, medicine, cell behavior, nutrition scientists employees in the world. In the area of micro-gravity science, the ISS has been central to the understanding of many phenomena in life sciences and technology.

In the area of human flight element of the European space program. It has become a reliable facility, with experiments that can be planned with experiments that can be planned with some confidence of execution. Fields now covered include micro-gravity research, medical and engineering sciences, chemistry, material developments, and fluid physics with the number of experiments carried out having increased substantially over recent years. The European program for life and physical sciences has produced many advanced in a variety of scientific disciplines since its inception in 2001 year, since the bulk of the substantial infrastructure costs for in the past, its use for science, which has been greatly improved in recent years, should continue to be optimized.

Thus, European space exploration human strategic plan can't only concentrate on flight (aviation) technology space professionals. It needs to seek other professionals, such as medical, psychology, science, biology, cell science, environment protection, life science , chemistry etc. professionals. Because this organization's mission is not only space science exploration, it includes other are related to space exploration research. If European space exploration only concentrate on researching space exploration, it will have risk , due to it spends existing funding be diverted from robotic missions to the intrinsically, even more expensive human space exploration program, single space exploration is much risk more than variety space exploration, e.g. space medicine, space medical, space tourism, space nature resource exploration, space cells exploration etc. different related space exploration businesses. Thus, strategic plan can't only concentrate on Moon or Mars space exploration . Because space has much potential business opportunities to let human to discover to gain any new business benefits to human.

In the future, human space exploration possible mission will include: defining the infrastructure priorities for servicing and cargo transportation whether by Ariane 5, by Soyuz launched from Centre Spatial Guyanais (CSG) , or by other commercial vehicles, strategically maintaining the options for human access to low Earth orbit more effective exploitation of the ISS for the physical , life science, engineering science and by the scientific community more generally (for example, involving announcements of opportunity for engineering sciences, articulating the role of the ISS in terms of human biology, especially in the context of future missions to the Moon or Mars, defining more what the ISS can contribute to the long term development of human space flight (such transportation systems, robot-human interfaces, and advanced life-support systems, expanding and enhancing its capabilities for education , which the astronauts on board have undertaken with great success, and further publishing its scientific work and potential.

Finally, how to reduce risk cost to space exploration, as soon as human space flight is considered the currently accepted wisdom is that risk to human life (in terms of launchers, survival systems, space tool and return to Earth) must be suppressed to extremely low levels of profitability. For example, the lowing possibility of a factor from 10% to 1% might increase the cost by a factor of 10 or more, but whether the formal probability estimates, significant advances in space exploration will always carry some risk to human life quantifying these risks will always be. However, difficult but a comparison with the historical levels of risk as commercial aviation development might provide a useful guide. Thus, why not single space exploration business (related space science businesses) can reduce risk as well as European and other countries space exploration cooperation can bring human benefits more than European (single) space exploration business investment. Thus, global strategic human resource plan must be need to European space exploration business.

Why does organizational development need strategic plan? Strategic plan is similar with a pyramid planning. At the low level of strategies/ tactics operations: How will the organization accomplish its goals? At the middle level of goals/objectives direction: what does the organization want to achieve? At the top level of principles beliefs: What does the organization mission and purpose? Why does the organization exist?

A well-developed strategic plan describes a vision for the future, strengths and weaknesses of the organization, the nature of the changes for sustainable growth and development, the sequence of these changes, those who are responsible for guiding change, the resources required, whether which currently exist within the organization or must be generated from external resources.

In a strategic plan, it consists mission , such as what we hope to accomplish , capabilities, resources, strengths and weaknesses, such as what you are capable of doing. Opportunities and threats , include needs of clients, and stakeholders, competitors and social , economic , political and technological forces. When all elements combine the strategic plan can be the fit. Long term strategic plan needs usually 5 to 10 years, focuses of future achievement, weighs a series of alternatives to make choices, resources mobilization with activities, operational plan needs short term (one year or less) , achievement to targets annual, alternatives are not considered, tend focus one unit or related such of activities, no formal action.

The direction between business
and tactic models and tactics

Nowadays, business model has been used by strategy to refer to the logic of the firm, the way it operates and how it creates value for its stakeholders. What is the relationship between business model and strategy? Can business model reflect a clear separation between tactics and strategy. This distinction is possible because strategy and business model are different constructs.

Any strategy can help a firm to learn to analyze its competitive environments defined its position, develops competitive corporate advantages and understands threats to sustaining advantage in the face of challenging competitive threats. However, external environment changing (variable) factor can influence a firm's development. Such as globalization, deregulation to technological change. So, any firm can't neglect to change to compete differently and innovate in its business model. For examples, IBM computer firm's 2006 year and 2008 year " Global CEO study", showed that top management in a broad range of computer industries are actively seeking guidance on how to innovate to its computer business model to improve its ability to both create and capture value.

Advances in information and communication technologies have driven the recent interest on business model innovation. Many e-businesses constitute new business models. Of course, not all business model innovations are IT driven; other forces , such as globalization and deregulation, have also resulted in new business models and fed the interest on this area. In fact, socially motivated enterprises that aim to reach the bottom of the pyramid constitute an important source of business model innovations. In truth, there is not yet agreement on what are the distinctive features of super business models. We believe that the dispute has arisen, because of lack of clear distinction between the strategy and business model and tactics.

Business model refers to the logic of the firm, the way, it operates and how it creates value of its stakeholders. Strategy refers to the choice of business model through which the firm will compete in the marketplace. Tactics refers to the residual choices open to a firm by the business model that it employs. What is the difference between the concepts of strategy , business models and tactics? In the first stage, firms need to choose a login of value creation and value capture (chose their business model). In the second stage, firms make tactical choices guided by their goals (in most cares, goals expect some form of stakeholder value maximization). So, the object of strategy is the choice of business model and the business model employed determines the tactics available to the firm to compete against, or cooperate with other firms in the marketplace. However, any business needs to know how the connection between strategy and business model and tactics can be clearly separated.

How to define a good business model? Two questions need to concern to answer : who is the customer and what does the customer value? what is the economic to customers at an appropriate cost? My idea is that business model refers to the logic by which that any business model should answer, one related to related to the value provided to the customer and the other to the organization's ability to capture value in the process of serving customers. For example, e-business can be an innovative technological business model to value chain analysis, the resource-based view of the firm, dynamic capabilities, transaction cost economies and strategic network. So, why business model is the first stage to design before strategy and tactics achievement.

Business model is similar to machine logic of operation system: any machine has a particular logic of operation (the way, the different components are assembled and related to one another), it runs in a particular way and in operating, it creates value for whomever uses it. For example, every automobile has a particular logic of operation, conventional automobiles operate quite differently than hybrids, and standard transmission automobiles. Different automobile models create different value for their stakeholders, the drivers. Some drivers may prefer standard transmission. Others may prefer a small car that allows them to easily navigate the streets of a congested city, others may prefer a powerful explosion engine to enjoy the countryside to the fullest. Different operation and create different value for their drivers. Likewise, to better understand business models, one needs to look at their component parts and understand how who relate to one another: The question arises: What are business models made of? I contend that business models are composed of two different elements. The concrete choices are made by management on how the organization must operate and the consequences of the choices both.

In fact, choices may include compensation, policy, contracts decision making, outsourcing decision, location of facilities, assets employed, extent of vertical integration, or sale and marketing methods. Every choice has consequence. For example, the provision of high-powered incentives (a choice) has implications regarding the willingness to exert effort or to cooperate with workers (consequences). Likewise, pricing policies (choices) regard sale volumes, affect the economies of scale and bargaining power is enjoyed by the firm both (two consequences).

In strategic plan view point, I indicate three types of choices: polices, assets and governance structure. Policies refer action that the firm adopts for all aspects of its operation, e.g. unions complain dealing, locating plants in rural or city areas choice, encouraging employees to fly tourist class, providing fee shares, bonus monetary incentives, or flying to secondary airports as a way to cut expenses to employee welfare. Asset refers to tangible resources, such as manufacturing facilities, a satellite system for communicating between offices or the use of a particular aircraft model by an airline. Governance of assets and policies refers to the structures of contractual arrangements that confer decision rights for policies or assets. For example, a given business model may contain as a choice to the certain assets, such as a fleet of tracks. The firm can own the fleet or lease it from a third part. The transaction cost economies can reduce the firm to pay asset purchase expenditure at same time because it only pay rent to lease to the fleet of trucks per month.

So, business model is as the logic of the firm, the way , it operates and how it creates value for its stakeholders. The make operational , we argue that business models are composed of choices (policies, assets, governance) and the consequences derived from the choices. For example, Ryanair airline business model includes: flying to secondary airports as lowest ticket prices, low commissions to travel agents, standardized fleet of Boeing 737s,treating all passengers equally, high powered incentives, none meals, nothing free. Consequences of these choices are: secondary airport changes low airport fees, lowest ticket prices can sell large volume, low commissions cost charges to travel agents, standardized fleet of Bosing 737 s has bargaining power with suppliers, all passengers treated equally to achieve economic of scale, high powered incentives to attract combative team, none meals provision to cause faster turnaround, nothing free causes addition revenue, headquarter is low fixed cost, and no unions will be flexibility.

Ryanair airline business model is similar to a machine is assembled and how it works. There are many ways in which a machine to performance a given task can be designed and assembled: Different levels of specific mechanisms, quality of components. Different machine have different direct consequences to affect the overall level of efficiency of the machine (speed, input, efficiency, noise, quality of output) etc. Other airlines are assembled differently than Ryanair airline , which have a different logic , a different way to operate and to create value for their stakeholders. These different ways to put together airlines correspond to different business models. In the case of Ryanair airline, the business model will have three cycles. The first cycle is : The lowest fares causes low quality service expected, to cause none meals, to cause low variable cost and to cause the consequence of lowest fares fare. The second cycles is: The lowest fare causes large volume, to cause high aircraft utilization, to cause low fixed cost/passenger, and to cause the consequence of lowest fares again. The third cycle is: The lowest fares causes large volume, to cause bargaining power with supplier, to cause low fixed fares again.

It is important to evaluate different cycles consequences. If the consequences are valuable , cycles develop valuable resources and capabilities. For example, as Ryanair airline's volume increases because of its low fares, bargaining power with its suppliers (airport authorities, Boeing, Airbus) grows resulting in improvement in Ryanair airline's advantage.

In fact, every organization has some business models. This is because organization makes some choices and these choices have the some consequences. Of course, this does not mean that every business model is satisfactory or even viable in long run. Some authors indicated business model has four elements: a customer value proposition, a profit formula, key resources ,and key processes. So, business model can articulate the value proposition. It can identify a market segment, if can define the structure of the value chain. It can estimate the cost structure and profit potential. How business model design involves assessment with respect to determine. It includes that the identify of market segment to be targeted, the benefits to rise to the enterprise will deliver to the clients, the technologies and features that are of the product and service, how the revenue and cost structure of a business design to meet client need, the way in which technologies are to be offered to the client. So, every organization will choose to decide how to determine the logic of the firm , the way in operates and how it creates value for its shareholders.

Tactics refers to the residual choices open to a firm of the business model that it employs. For example, for newspaper publishing's choice of tactics. A newspaper publishing firm can't change price of the newspaper because its business model is ad-sponsored and the newspaper must be sold at zero price. Put differently the newspaper publishing business model precludes from using "price of the newspaper" as a variable that can be changed depending on the intensity of competition and other external factors. Thus, price of the newspaper is not part of the newspaper publishing business's set of tactics. For another example, some business school for MBA student, every student gets a personalized MBA curriculum, depending on whose background and professional goals. Some business schools used in many of the school's executive education programs with several faculty members co-teaching the core courses and with assets, such as classrooms, with set up for case discussions for large groups educational method; another some business schools are impossible to provide similar education methods which business model do not have as an element in whose tactical set the offering of a tailored MBA course.

These business schools modify whose businesses models. So that those tactical choices would become available, but with the current businesses models, which are not possible for them to match the other business schools' similar business models for education method to MBA course. We conclude that different business models give rise to different tactics available for competition and /or cooperation. However, tactical play an important role in determining how and value is created and captured by firms. For newspaper publishing industry example, advertising rates and the precise number of ads. displayed in the free newspaper and up affecting the readership and advertising revenues. So, likewise, of some free charge newspaper publishing's advertising rate increases, fewer advertisers with want to advertise in these free charge newspaper publishing's revenue, profit and value capture. Therefore, not only the business model employed by the firm determines factor, but also tactics play a central role in how much value the firm will be able to create and capture of the end of the day. Tactical interaction refers to the way organizations affect each other by acting within the bounds set by their business models. Using this imagery of business model, representations, tactical interaction occur when one firm's business model is in contact will that of another firm. When this happens, there are consequences in both firms business models, where feedback to be determined not only by the focal firms choices, but by the choices of the other firm as well. For a discount retailer store example, it competes with another local retailer store, both engage in a tactical pricing competition to win customers. The interaction between the discounted and the non-discounted retailer stores can be captured to display both business models connected at market share. In this example of discount retailer stores and non-discount retailer stores, when both stores use prices in their tactical interaction. The discount retailer stores bring superior weapons to fight because of the business model that it employs to compete.

Specially, the range of prices, discount retailer stores can profitably set is much broader the profitability other non-discount retailer store competitors with a high cost operating model. So, the non-discount retailer stores can choose to sell the products or foods at higher or non-discounted price. When the discount retailer stores lack to sell whose same of similar products or foods. It means cooperation retail method of tactical interaction will be needed in this store retail market.

Strategy is often defined as a contingent plan of action designed to achieve a particular goal. Strategy is the creation of a unique and valuable position, involving a different set of activities. Creation implies choice of the particular way in which the firm competes. So, strategy is not the activity system itself, but the creation of the activity system itself, but the creation of the activity system. So, strategy refers in our development, for the contingent plan as to what business model to use. Strategy in a higher order choice that has profound implications on competitive outcomes. Choosing a particular business model means choosing a particular way to compete, a particular logic a particular way to compete, a particular logic of the firm, a particular way to operate and to create value for the firm's stakeholders. For example, model means choosing a particular way to compete, particular logic of the firm, a particular way to operate and to create value for the firm's stakeholders. For Ryanair airline example, it was encountering bankruptcy in the early 1990 year, its strategy was a plan of action to transform its airline business model from that of a standard full-service (through small) airline to a radically different one by adopting the Southwest's no-frills business model. In the mid 1990 year , after the transformation had taken place, Ryanair airline strategy. Ryanair 's top management considered four alternative plans of action to solve bankruptcy challenge. (1) becoming the Southwest of Europe, (2) Adding business class , (3) Becoming a feeder airline operating from Shannan 's airport, or (4) Existing the airline industry. Each of the entailed a different business model, a different logic of the airline firm, the way , it operates and how it creates value for its stakeholder. The high level election of becoming the Southwest of Europe (as opposed to adding business class or operating as a feeder airlines was strategy (a plan of action to create a unique and valuable position, involving a different set of activities).

Furthermore, the particular way in which Ryanair airline executed such plans was its realized strategy. The resulting new Ryanair airline with its new logic, new way to operate, and new way to create value for its stakeholders , was business model. What is the different between business model and strategy? A firm's business model is a reflection of its realized strategy. What do organization gain from having two separate concepts. There is the choice of business model because, there is a over time mapping from strategy onto business models. This means business model, an outside observer knows the firm's strategy. Some authors felt the substantive different between strategy and business models arises when the firm's plan of action calls for modifications to the business model (changes in policies and/or assets and/or governance) when particular contingencies take place. However, there are many possible sources of contingencies upon which strategies may be based. One such source is the realization of an event outside the control of the firm. For example, one contingency the many firm are currently considering is the possibility of a recovery from the recession. Firms have plans as to how their business models must be kept of a strong economic recovery (changes in polities, asset, and/or governance).

Such as plans are part of firms' strategies.

How will business model be changes by firm's strategy? What is a strategy in this economic recession situation? so, business model is prior to achieve any strategic plans. It is a logic organization design or mind to prepare to achieve any strategic plans as well as tactical operation plans. Has it difference between strategy and strategic management? When reviewing strategic thinking , using realize how this phenomenon differs in any organizations. In military view point, strategy can be used in a military campaigns. It means a way of prevailing over the adversary, a fool of victory i war . In organization view point, strategy can be applied to human relations, political, economics, business. The concept of strategy has evolved into a field of knowledge in management. Otherwise, strategy management, with content, concepts and practical reasoning, role in the academic and business fields.

Whether do concept of strategy and strategic management are understood by business managers? What is strategy and strategic management to future managers? Are who understood and recognized? To answer these two questions? We need to seek these specific objectives. (i) To build a model explaining the definition of strategy (ii) To identify which concept of strategic management in the literature. To understand these difference of two concepts. We need to adopt organizational phenomenon in different situations. In this case, the development of organizational strategy depends on what strategy and strategic management depend on understanding the perceptions of their managers on what strategy and strategic management actually is. It concerns how to predict consumer behaviors. In the field of strategy, managers represent an innovation, and a new alternative for research.

Strategy and strategic management concepts can be explained what differ from historical perspective. In any enterprises, creating and managing strategic enable them to meet the challenges of the market, reaching their objectives in the short, medium and long term. Strategic concerns great development within the corporate environment. Phenomena , such as corporate restructuring , joint decisions and actions impacting on organization size, financing were driven by the technological advance in means of communication and transport and an interactive dynamic global level have become predominant. Nowadays, thinking strategically has acquired the status of a factor in leading and managing organizations, whether for profit or otherwise. After all, strategy addresses the link between the inner world of business and its external environment.

Considering strategy is as a business logic rational and sequential, to the most dynamic that understand this process is as associated with cultural and learning factors, political and power relations. Strategy is not only one way of dealing in competition environment or market, as treated not only summarize the ideas, proposal, guidelines, indicative of paths and solutions. It has the concept of operational efficiency. In summary, strategy is what matters for the effectiveness of the organization, the external point of view, which stresses the research of the objectives against the environment, in term of internal stresses, the balance communication between members of the organization and a willingness contribute towards actions and the achievement of the common objectives; it is a series of actions to a particular situation, it is analyzing the present situation and changing it whenever necessary. It is the determinant of the basis long term goals of a firm and the adoption of action how to allocate resource necessary for carrying out these goals; it is a rule for making decisions determined by product/market scope, growth competitive advantage and synergy, it is addition of the decisions taken by an organization in all aspects , as much commercial as structural with the learning process to management, it is the directional action decisions to achieve firm's objectives. Hence, strategy is long term or short term plan to aim to achieve any missions or objectives for any organizations.

Otherwise, strategic management defines key attributes: directed towards the overall organization objectives, includes multiple stakeholders in decision making, requires incorporating short and long term perspectives and involves the recognition of trade offs between effectiveness and efficiency. Strategy management is as an ongoing process involving the efforts of strategic managers to adjust the organization to the environment in which it operates when developing competitive advantages. These competitive advantages enable the company to seize opportunities and minimize environmental threats. It is a broad term that includes determining the mission and objective of the organization in the external and internal environment.

Strategic communication plan

How can organizational communication influence effectiveness and efficiency? What are the most effective pathways for delivering organizational messages to priority audiences? Is it the suitable media? Face-to-face meeting? Direct mail? The internet ? How will organization deliver message efficiently?

Without a plan to guide organizational communication activities, the organization runs the risk of focusing on the wrong audiences, of using messages that simply do not work. In other words, without a well-thought-through plan, your organization runs the risk of becoming irrelevant with key audiences, even of failing to meet organizational mission.

How to strategic communication plan? Your organization needs to proactively focus the activities of your organization, where there is the greatest potential for success; ensures your limited resources (time and financial most effectively applied) imposes discipline and clear thinking about why it is the best interest for your communication method to your organization to pursue certain communication initiatives; to integrate all of your public relations efforts; media, government, donor to corporate etc. ; to ensure that every member in your organization staff board, volunteers are on the same level fairly, to achieve results that more your members towards realizing your organization's goals and to encourage creative thinking about new ways to address old challenges.

So, communication plan is simply a written statement that outlines communication goals, provides some situational analysis and proposes approaches and activities to achieve the identified goals given the identified current situation. An effective communication plan can be set out the timeframe for carrying and these activities, details the resources and supports that will be necessary to achieve your organizational goals, and identifies how results will be measured. It can be a summary document of only a few pages or a 40 pages on more. Part of length and depth of a plan depends on whether it is a five year organizational plan or a plan designed to support a particular campaign or strategic goal.

In the private and government sectors, communication plans are typically development on support of detailed organizational strategic plan. In the non-profit aim organization sector, it is most common to see strategic communication plans as a organizational and communication planning processes. An effective strategic communication plan focuses on many different ways of reaching all of the external and internal audiences, your organization will need to hear your messages.

How to create communication plan for your organization to improve: the ability to create a strong and positive reputation for your organization and public relations; building relationship and reputation with the media and with reputation with government at all levels; building relationship with employees and volunteer, e.g. internal communications; ability to attract an maintain strong donor support relations; building sponsorship and funding opportunities with business corporate relations; building organization's policies and direction board-staff relations; outreach about programs and services (constituency any client relations).

How to build morals within team by communication plan? Establishing goals to staff and volunteers, understanding every staff can meet is energized and ready to take on more ambitious goals. Communication plan aims to effective facilities meetings, a creative brainstorm and a focus group. Organizing effective communication plan has these stages: Stage one includes that defining organization goals, defining communication objectives, situation analysis to organizational background and external environment. Stage two includes that determining who your organizational audiences are and what messages are delivered before you move to messages. Stage three determining what your organization strategies , what tactics are. Stage four, evaluation of ideas for strategies and tactics, implementation budget before investing time in developing the timing and timeline sections, identifying certain strategic and tactics resources, producing multiple communication opportunities having a communication plan will make it easier to determine whose to allocate limited resources.

How to develop strategic environment plan? It will largely be determined by the level of buy-in that key staff and board have for the plan. Buy-in is easiest to achieve when staff have had a role in developing the plan and feel some level of ownership of ideas contained within it. All of the pieces of a communication plan are represented in the following pages. They have been laid and in a logical order by moving from organizational goals to situation analysis to audiences and messages.

Reasons need strategic plan

Why organizations need strategic plan

American Management Association defines and differentiates between strategy, policy and objective. It indicates that policies get procedures into roles. Strategies get into tactics, resulting in an-end-means. For example, it supposes a company decides upon a sales growth of between 35 and 45 per cent and desires to achieves this by acquiring other companies, instead of introducing new products, instead of introducing new products. So, it seems strategic plan can help organization has ability to predict how to achieve its strategy to achieve sale growth aim.

For example, acquisition can be considered as a strategy is chosen by the company. The company will then have to decide on the size of the firm to be required. If it decides on acquiring a small company. This becomes the objectives. In general, strategy means the determination of the basic long term goals and objectives of an enterprise and the adoption of the action and the allocation of resources necessary for carrying out these goals.

In micro organization view, strategy is the pattern of objectives and plans for achieving these goals, purposes and goals and the major policies and plans for achieving these goals stated in such a way, so it is defined what business, the company is in or is to be and the kind of company, it is or is to be. Also, some authors define a strategy is a set of decision-making rules for the guidance of organizational behaviors. Because firm's internal and external environment change over time, the strategy also changes consequently, the idea that strategy is dynamic.

Otherwise, in macro organization view, strategic management is a science of choosing the alternatives from the designed and available actions. The managers have to decide on a process that will be most suitable to their conditions and what could enable them to achieve a desired position of their organization in overall. Large organizations which use detailed strategic management models whereas smaller businesses concentrate on planning steps compared to larger companies in the same industry. In short, the most highly rated benefits of strategic management are: charity of strategic vision for the organization, focus on what is strategically important to the organization, better understanding of the rapidly changing business environment.

What is strategic management?

How can strategic management assist organizational development? Some management psychologists indicate any large organizational participant members needed to be trained a widely varying traditions, some in economic departments, some in strategic management departments, some is organizational behavior, some in marketing etc. departments. Trained strategic management organizations can be more efficiently and effectively to compare to non-trained strategic management organizations.

Exactly what is it? Strategic management owning organizations can know how to raise internal strengths and reduce internal weaknesses as well as can know how to predict or avoid external threats occur and absorb or raise opportunities more easily.

Strategic management can be assumed that scientific knowledge is socially constructed and is the fundamental medium that makes that social construction possible. What are the differences between strategic management organization and non strategic organization? We were interested in identifying the fundamental definition , not the monetary fashions or cycles of the field, such as micro-organizational behavior or human resource to explain what differences are between of them.

In an effort to distinguish strategic management organizations from other subfields of management organizations, consideration of how strategic management differs from or relates to other academic fields, such as economy, marketing or sociology. We would have liked to include strategy-oriented organizations from these other related field, but which are too rare to allow the type of analysis we conducted.

Has it relationship between strategic management and top management team, capital intensity and market structure. We need to examine these existing definitions and comparing them to conceptual categories. Some management professionals defined strategic management is as imputed from the distinction of the field: The field of strategic management deals with the major intended and emergent initiatives, involving utilization of resources, enhancing the performance to their external environments. They also indicated six elements make up the definition of the fields of strategic management. The first definitional element is the major intended and emergent initiatives, such as strategy, acquisition and diversification, which refer to relatively deliberate, planned initiatives, but it also includes such as learning, and innovation, which represent the move emergent activities that occur in a firm. The second definitional element is taken by general managers on behalf of owners to concern the key actors who are the focus of attention strategy research. Terms such CEO, directors, board represents the upper level. The third definitional element is involving utilization of resources that managers use in their strategic initiatives, e.g. capability and knowledge represent the resources that are internal to the firm, whereas, terms , such primarily as ties resources that link the firm to its environment and the performance. The fourth element is enhanced the performance, conceptualizes the key objectives or outcomes that are of interest to strategic management scholars, e.g. growth performance to achieve advantages. The fifth definition element indicates firms which reflects the focal unit of analysis of strategic management. Finally, the sixth element is in their external environments and is represented by market competitor and industry, which refer to the immediate environment of a firm as well as by uncertainty environment contingency, which indicate a potentially broader external context.

Porter Michael (1986) , long time Harvard professor and editor of the Harvard Business Review, published the first edition of the competitive strategy, who explained "strategy means the pattern of decision in a company that determines and reveals its objective purposes or goals, produces the principal policies and plans for achieving these goals, and defines the range of business the company is to pursue, the kind of economic and human organization, it is or intends to be, and the nature of the economic and non-economic contribution it intends to make to its shareholders, employees, customers, and communities".

In the military, the strategy for a battle refers to a general plan of attack or defense. In civil terms, strategy is concerned with the deployment of resources, this is amounts to the allocation of resources. Tactics, then is concerned with the employment of resources already deployed. In the civilian sector, this equates to operations in the board sense of the terms. Generally speaking, tactical re-expected to occur in the context of strategy, so as to ensure the attainment of strategic intent. However, strategy can fail end, when it does tactics dominate the action. Execution becomes strategy. Thus, it is always one part intended (the plan as conceived beforehand) and one part emergent (on adaption to the conditions encountered). As a consequence, there are always two versions of a given strategy: (1) strategy is as intended and (2) strategy (c) realized.

In fact, a strategy or general plan of action might be formulated for broad, long-term corporate goals and objectives, for more specific business goals and objectives, or for a functional unit, even one as small as a cost center. Such goals might or might not cause the nature of the organization, its culture. The kind of company its leadership wants it to be the markets, it will or won't enter. The basic on which it will compete or any other attribute quality or characteristic of the organization. Because strategies can do exist at various levels of the organization, it is conceivable and appropriate for the corporation to have a strategic plan , for a business unit to have one too, and for a functional unit to have one. Strategic plan can import to all organizational levels. So, it is intended to address matters of great importance. For those concerned with the enterprise, strategic issues, initiatives and plans are those that affect the entire enterprise is important ways. So the top, middle and low levels ought need to have short term and long term strategic plans to implement.

What is the direction and destination of the firm? Where is it headed and what is it to become? Not all strategic issues are long term, although may be. A short term crisis can be of strategic significance and should be dealt with accordingly.

Plans of action, whether for business always have two fundamental aspects: ends and means . What is to be achieved and how it is to be achieved? What are the firm's future results, e.g. goals, aims , targets or objectives consequences . Firms can choose either program or action or step or initiative to achieve enterprise level or business unit level or functional level future result. Those combination of ends and means firm can find any plans in all these levels of organizations. Strategies are too exist at all three levels. Consequently, one can and should find strategic thinking, planning and management at all three levels.

However, planning has been defined in various ways, ranging from thinking about the future to specifying in advance who is to do what and when. For firm plan, it can define the activity of preparing a plan, a set of intended outcomes (ends). Planning can be formal or informal , an involve lots of documentation or very little. The information base can be large and captured in a wide range of reports, studies, databases and analyses, or it can rest entirely on the personal knowledge of a few people or even just one. Plans and thus the planning activities that produce them, frequently with address timeframe, either generally or in the form of perhaps detailed schedules, resources too, might be addressed, whether in terms of money, space, equipment or people. There are no predetermined guideline to follow, it is a matter of doing what is appropriate for the task at hand.

In conclusion, strategic planning characteristics includes: establishing and periodically confirming the organization's mission and its corporate strategy what has been termed the contest for managing ; setting strategic or enterprise level financial and non-financial goals and objective; developing broad plans of action necessary to attain these goals and objectives; allocating resources on a basis consistent with strategic directions and goals and objectives and managing the various lines of business as an investment portfolio; deploying the mission and strategy. That is articulating and communicating it, as well as developing action plans at lower levels that are supportive of those at the enterprise level , one very specific method of policy or strategy deployment; monitoring results, measuring progress, and making such adjustments as are required to achieve the strategic intent specified in the strategic goals and objectives; reassessing mission, strategy, strategic goals and objectives and plans at all levels and if requires , revising any or all of them.

Why needs strategic versus
non-strategic cooperation
On reason why organization needs strategic plan because it can not revist to compare whether what it can improve or change to be better between the strategic cooperation stage and non-strategic cooperation stage if it choose to achieve strategic plan. What are the difference between strategic cooperation and non-strategic cooperation within any organizations? What are the benefits to strategic cooperation organizations? The strategic motivations are in play in finitely repeated in any organizations. Clearly, cooperation can drop because strategically-motivated individuals, who reciprocate others' cooperation solely when there is future interaction. However, it can also drop because non-strategically-motivated individuals, who reciprocate others' cooperation even in the absence of future interaction, believe others will stop cooperating in the last period. In other word, since both strategically - and non-strategically motivated individuals can cause the decline in cooperation , it is difficult to know what the contribution of each type of motivation is. So, it seems that if any organization can review to measure any staff individual motivated effect with team cooperation, it will improve strategic plan to be more successfully or more better to compare prior year and current year strategic plans.

Some psychologists have done this experiment, for example, one team member could take the increase in cooperation between repeated games and (repetitions of) one short game as being caused by strategically -motivated individuals who now have a reason to cooperate. However, this increase can also be driven by non-strategically-motivated individuals who cooperate more because who expect that within repeated interaction others will be more cooperative. Similarly, the observation that cooperation is more frequent when it is more profitable can be attributed to strategic behavior and the existence of additional cooperative equilibria. However, the increase in cooperation can able be , due to an increase in non-strategically-motivated cooperation that results from intrinsically-motivated individuals who now find cooperation relatively more attractive or from rational individual who make relatively more mistakes.

How to distinguish strategic from non-strategic motivations for cooperation in organizations? Psychologists conclude that strategic behavior has a more pronounced effect than learning in explaining the usually-observed decline in contributions in public good games. On the basis of experiment treatments, who observed cooperation is strategically motivated. However, the relative importance of non-strategic motivations increases with the profitability of cooperation. So, psychologists indicate different organization departments cooperation can encourage individual staff motivations after strategic cooperation. Otherwise, non-strategic cooperation different departments will be more unsuccessful. It seems that how to encourage department cooperation factor which can influence the organization can raise productivity or improve service performance more easily.

Strategic plan tangible and
intangible benefits

Why will inefficient and effective strategic plan bring disadvantages or lack benefits to any organizations? Motivating staff and volunteers, thinking about the future is a stimulating and energizing process. It can create a shared vision, with ideas about how to achieve that vision. Building a planning team with a common vision. The strategy plan that emerges from the process is generally more realistic and achievable and working or interdependent relationships within the organization are strengthened. Confronting key issues and solving problems. Strategic planning sets in motion a dynamic process that allows the organization to continually reassess, confront change, and grow within an agreed-upon framework. Defining roles and responsibilities , measurable performance objectives are set and the person(s) who is responsible for specific activities is identified. Challenging the status, the process creates an open atmosphere. How can organization do things better in a more systematic and thorough way. Allowing busy managers and policy makers to concentrate on the organization's future for a short period of time, meaning that who will be able to focus their expertise and insights on self-assessment and planning future directions. Explaining organization to others , a thoughtful and clear strategic plan is often a good marketing tool and can encourage shares issues support for the organizational mission that individual perspectives, roles and problems are subsumed by an overall plan that coordinates all staff members and volunteers , so that agreed upon goals and objectives are achieved in a timely manner.

The steps of strategic plan suggesting: First step, analyzing the shared valued and experiences of staff and board. Planning a meeting or workshop to facilitate strategic planning. Second step, review and update or prepare a mission statement for the organization. Third step, analyzing the organization's external environment, political , economic, social and technological factors and internal environment: resources or input, processes, and performance or outputs. Fourth step, conducting a SWOT analysis (assessing the organization's internal strengths and weaknesses and its external opportunities and threats). Fifth step, creating smaller groups for in-depth planning activities in key areas. Sixth step, reviewing the organization's existing strategic plan if there is one to identify aspects of the plan that are still strategic, those are as longer strategic plan, due to changing environments, and gaps or new issues that should be addressed in a revised plan. Seventh step, outlining a vision of where the organization should be outlining three to five years from today (the vision of success). Eighth step, identifying the strategic issues facing the organization. Ninth step, formulating goals and strategic objectives to address major issues facing the organization and ensuring its longer term growth and sustainability. Tenth step, developing work plans showing specific activities, persons responsibility resources needed and indicators why which performance will be measured. Eleventh step, identifying next step for resource mobilization and creating a approaches for generating sufficient revenue funding. Twelve step, preparing the written detailed 5 years strategic plan mission statements. Final step, identifying next steps for resources mobilization and creating a financial plan that cost, and outlines approaches for sufficient revenue or funding .

Reference

Chovancova, M. (2012), " Building a strong brand to support company competitiveness"., from www.sba.org.pl.content/50647.

Davis, Gerald, 1991, " Agents without principles: The Spread Of The Poison Pill Through The Intercorporate Network." Administrative Science Quarterly, 36: 583-613.

Obembe, D. understanding individual action: whn employees contravence management directives to faster knowledge sharing. Management research review. 2010, vol. 33, issue. 6 , pp. 656-666. ISSN 2040-8269.

Poister, Theodore H. Streib, gregory (2005), "Elements of strategic planning and management in municipal government, Status after two decades", Public Administration Review, 65(1), pp.45.

Hickson, D. J. Miller, S.C. , Wilson , D.C. Planned on prioritized, implementation of strategic decisions. J. Manage, Stud , 2003, 40, 1803-1836.

Johnston, R., Clack, G., 2001. Service operations management, Prentice-Hall, Harlow, UK.

Kay, J.M. (2006). "Strong brands and corporate brands", European Journal Of Marketing, vol. 40, no.7/8, pp. 742-760.

Porter, Michael (1986). Competitive Strategies. Harvard Business School Press.

Shahri, M.H. (2011), " The effectiveness of corporate branding strategy in multi- business companies", Australia Journal of Business And Management Research, vol. 1 no 6, pp. 51-59.

Stanhope, M. & Lancaster, J. (2000). Community & Public Health, St. Louis, Mo, Mobsy.

Xie, Y.H. and Boggs, J.D. (2006), " corporate branding vs. product branding in emerging markets, a conceptual framework", Marketing intelligence & planning, vol. 24 no. 24, pp. 347-364.

CHAPTER THREE

UK AND US OUTSOURCED BUSINESS DEVELOPMENT

UK Future Unique Technology

Online teaching technology
Future, online teaching method will be popular to be applied to teach to any university, even secondary and primary schools. Because internet service is free charge to any students in any countries. Many different age students who can know how to apply internet as well as internet studying is very convenient to any students who can to internet to learn or study in home or public library or school library conveniently. Teachers do not need spend much time to teach students in classroom. They can use internet to teach teachers by face to face seeing and talking to their individual student from every student's computer. So, students do not also often spend much time to go to school to learn. So, developing any fast speed and time saving and talking and listening online teaching methods will be popular needs to any UK primary and secondary and university students in the future. It will be one new technological teaching method to change the traditional classroom educational method in UK and schools. For example, when one UK student who had left UK and is living in another country long time. If any UK school did not provide online teaching service to any UK students.

It means that the UK citizen can not choose study himself/herself any UK school if who still hope to study any UK course when who is living in another country. Even one foreign student who does not go to UK to study, if he/she can find any UK primary or secondary or university to study from online. Then, the UK school won't lose one foreign student, due to it does not provide online teaching method to any foreign students. So, online Technology educational learning method will be one popular learning method which is enhanced, supported, mediated or assessed by the use of electronic media. Technology also enhanced learning may involve the use of new or established technology and/or the creation of new learning material. It may be deployed both locally and at a distance (i.e. a combination of traditional and e-learning approaches), to learning that is delivered entirely online. Online learning technology characteristics (features) include identification of a project lead for each area of any learning strategy, identification of two " quick win" for example lecture capture, electronic submission and feedback.

How can online technology enhance learning at UK any schools? It will include these several aspects to analyze. On identifying, prioritizing and innovation hand, online technology is a process for resourcing, prioritizing, acquiring and evaluating school software and hardware for UK any school needs. On staff development learning plan and a student skills development plan hand, UK schools need to establish a base-line policy on the standard (minimum) technology enhanced learning expectation for education each program and module and a mechanism for updating the schools' policies. On evaluation and research hand, a mechanism for engaging the owners of the technology enhanced learning strategy with best practice in the sector including contributing to and benefiting from pedagogical research and the evaluation of the student experience to UK any school.

Thus, UK schools can apply online technology to develop on educational aspect, such as digital literacies and appropriate technical skills that equip UK students for life-long learning, graduate level employment and professional practice, be empowered to learn how to learn with online teaching technology, using online technology to engage in interactive, creative and co-constructed learning with the potential for online learning in an interdisciplinary and international context, using online teaching technology to engage in learning with and from people from anywhere in the world, be supported on placement and in workplace learning through mobile applications and other supportive technologies that facilitate their online learning when away from the classroom, having access to innovative methods of online learning teaching and assessment that are the foundation of a research-lead academic environment, engaging with UK schools in developing , implementing and reviewing the technology enhanced learning strategy. Thus, in the future, it is important to build a capacity to the online education strategy to adopt future learning innovation and student individual online learning need (demand) to UK any school online teaching trend.

There are many examples where UK academics working in isolation or in small UK teaching organizations or classroom learning groups have developed teaching innovation that have a positive impact on UK students' academic experience , but these have remained isolated to particular modules or occasionally program. The aim of education researching online learning process is to identify the good online teaching innovation that is being developed and to prioritize those that have the potential to make a significant contribution to improving the academic student experience at UK any schools. This online teaching process will need any UK schools which can plan how to apply limited resources necessary to achieve online teaching. In addition, the online teaching research process would evaluate and prioritize large scale educational software and hardware requests for primary, secondary and university students' requests. An important part to this process will be to ensure the integration of online educational products and packages that school staff and students regular use to make routine working and access as seamless as possible.

Decisions about school administrative online technologies should not be taken in isolation before assessing the impact on UK teaching staff. In addition, a range of techniques such as, online expert facilitation, coaching and peer support will be used to support individuals, groups or longer academic units, who are learning on major technology enhanced online learning projects. Staff engagement may also facilitated through incorporating technology that is used in teaching staff research and/or professional activity that can be cooperated into their teaching.

Online learning technology can develop UK students skills, UK schools need to understand how UK students understand technology and learn with it, therefore the digital literacy strategy needs to be considered as part of the overall strategy as well as the relevant skills development in UK employability strategy. So, in the future, online learning strategy will make it clear that students will develop technical skills the appropriate level for graduate employability and professional practice. Also, in the future, the online technology can enhance learning working group to discuss external development, that are of educational strategic importance, understanding and evaluating current best practice and research and understanding and evaluating the online educational strategic contribution that pedagogical research and student feedback can have on online educational strategy, policy and practice. The e-learning unit is responsible for informing and educating. This could be done by, for example, providing a short digest of relevant information for each meeting and by setting aside a proportion of each school meeting to discuss a topic of particular online educational strategic interest to every school. Academics that have not got a specialist interest in online educational technology enhanced learning will need relevant information at an appropriate time. This could be provided at a school department or faculty level and this will have clear links to the staff online teaching development plan. Hence, online educational development strategy will influence any UK educational school technological improvement in the future.

Environmental protection technology

Why does environment technology valid to UK businessmen and government to develop? Nowadays, global air and water pollution is serious. Even, UK has many farming is polluted by the water and air pollution. It will influence UK farmers' income if whose farm land (natural resource) is polluted by water or air (natural resource). Even it will influence UK citizen will encounter food shortage if UK farmers can not grow any fresh and health food to provide the enough food numbers to eat every day. Moreover, air and water pollution will influence UK citizen drink the polluted water and breathe the dirty air to live every day. This natural resource (air and water challenge) will influence UK citizen health to cause illness , even death every easily. So, UK government can not neglect the natural environment pollution challenge. The environmental protection technology will help the UK and development countries to solve the challenge of climate change to avoid or reduce farming, foods, or vegetable or fruits or rice, pork, livestock numbers loss threats, i.e. the development and deployment of low carbon energy technology, including technology for the efficient use of energy. The commercialization of low carbon energy and energy efficiency technologies in the UK, with a specific focus on the demonstration and deployment phases of bringing low carbon technologies to UK market.

The UK Government needs to deliver a low carbon economy and to meet UK ambitions emission reduction target. So, low carbon and environmental protection technology researching and development will reduce the carbon intensity of energy production as well as reduce energy demand, towards meeting the contributing UK's ambitions production as well as reduce energy demand, and renewable energy goals. The use of energy (including transportation fuel) and the UK's targets on climate change, for example, by helping the UK make a step change in increasing deployment of renewable energy, improving UK energy efficiency and helping low carbon technologies reach the market. The development of low carbon technologies, and to realize the benefits of doing so in terms ensuring security of energy supply for the UK future economy development.

In UK, private sector investment in technology innovation in the low carbon energy sector will other sectors of the economy. So, in UK energy technologies are likely needed to be developed to avoid dangerous climate change, or an acceptable cost. So, in the future, UK government will need to consider to research environment protection and low carbon energy technology. The activities will reduce carbon emissions, or have the potential to reduce carbon emissions on the longer term, through the use of energy technology will accelerate development and deployment of low-carbon energy and energy efficiency technologies will capacity in the demonstration and deployment of low carbon technologies. Innovation in the energy sector is the only way to identify, develop and reduce the costs of new and improved technologies for the extractions, generation, distribution and use of energy. It has long been an important means of achieving the UK's energy policy aims of a secure and affordable energy supply, as well as to develop the environmentally friendly technologies that are required in UK response to climate change, i.e. nuclear, wind or water, sun energy technology, which is future new energy technology is suitable to research to create to apply instead of current electricity energy.

How global warming influences UK agriculture growth. Scientists have also been fighting the use of chlorine in municipal water systems to kill various strands of bacteria. Chlorine reduces by about 80% the number of alimentary tract diseases relative to polluted, unchlorinated water. A relatively new genetically modified agricultural products. They were partly successful in Europe, such as UK (some countries banned genetically modified products) in spite of the fact that neither history nor research supports their case. People began to modify plants as early as the beginning of the agricultural revolution (8000 to 10,000 years ago), when they started seed selection and who have continued ever since. The green revolution of the 1960 year brought about strains of grans and rice more resistant to a variety of local conditions. The effects have been that countries like India, which had suffered from recurrent famines over the millennia, became self-sufficient in food due to the resultant sharp increase in agricultural productivity. It was a real science and technology over the poverty dominating most of human history. But it is precisely the products of science and technology that ecologists are so deathly afraid of. In an interesting study in a quarter (28%) of clinically analyzed cases of obsessive compulsive disorder were cases resulting from the fear of global warming.

To destroy the modern, whether industrial or postindustrial, civilization, human have to destroy an important engine of economic growth, that is its energy sources. And this is what eco-warriors try to achieve under the banner of against global warming. Thus, UK government will have responsibility to attempt to research new technology to fight global warming challenge for itself farmer benefits and even global benefits both on the future.

● Future Economist global warming technological protection economic influence opinion

Some future economists indicated reasons to explain why UK government and businessmen needed to consider how to develop natural environment protection technology to avoid global warming challenge to influence UK economy development. They indicated the anthropogenic (human-made) global warming resulting from the increase in "greenhouse gas". They offered their perspectives on the scientific valid of anthropogenic global warming phenomenon, its probability of occur and expected consequences and is dominated by technologists, economists and political scientists, who considered the need to make the horribly costly adjustments in energy generation and usage suggested by climate alarmists.

Many stress that global warming is primarily caused by other phenomena than human use of fossil fuels or human activities in general. They are looking at the activities of the sun and impact of the larger universe as the main source of global warming and stress that global warmings (plural) happen intermittently with global cooling. I shall explain why global climate warming will influence to the political and economics of the issue to UK country. For it is the latter, rather than the global warming itself, that will pose a challenge to the Western world, such as UK and the world at large in the future. Scientists concerned who should move forward with policy measures to avert the alleged disaster. They also apply manufacturing theories to support enough to frighten politicians into action and scare societies into acceptance of measures that would sharply reduce UK citizen their living standards. Otherwise, UK politicians had support that bureaucracies were established, money allocated and lobbies created dependent on the new kind of subsidies. In consequences, climate alarmism and resultant interventions in national economies and human activities have become the increasingly wide spread and increasingly cost reality. With the growing availability of money distributed, and even more promised, a range of benefit of the global warming machinery has been on the increase. So, if UK government did not concern how to innovate new weather protection technology to avoid climate change adverse (poor) influence. It is possible that billions of dollars of UK public money are needed to spend on research global warming challenge because global warming will influence UK agricultural industry. UK agricultural industry is one important export income source to raise UK GDP income every year. If global warming become very serious to influence UK weather to be bad to cause UK farmers who can not grow good taste food and vegetable to supply to domestic and overseas food consumers to eat. Then, UK will loss much GDP income from local agricultural export sale. It seems global warming and agricultural production which has direct relationship to influence UK economy development in the future.

The main problem with climatology is that it must be based as already stressed on very many variables affecting climate and too few hard data necessity. Differences apply not only with respect to the scale of changes obtained, but even to their direction (rising or declining temperature). Some weather scientists indicated to concern global warming challenge. In consequence, it would be impossible to discover if and where errors were made not only in estimating relationships between variables but also in the quality of data used. (Hauser, J. Tellis, G. J; Griffin, A. 2006) They were comparing average temperatures measured some 30, 40 or 50 years ago by, say, 90 % weather stations in the countryside and 10 % stations in the cities with contemporary average temperatures measured by weather stations located today on 50:50 basis in the countryside and cities. Then, one could obtain the increasing temperatures without any real world climate or even weather changes. Comparability would be ensured if the same number of countryside-located and city-located weather stations had been compared for different periods. The alarmists intentionally mix up " temperature growth" with the trend of temperature growth. To give an example, if in the first decade the temperature grew by 0.5 % degree, in second decade it grew by 0.3 % and in third decade it grew by 0.1%, what was registered was a growth in the temperature, but certainly not a trend of growing temperature. A fourth decade should, on the basis of the trend, bring about no change in the temperature.

To conclude, scientists believed that global warming was caused by human's bad behavior more than natural environment influence. So, it is human's responsibility needs to solve this challenge, due to who feel earning profit aim is more important to protect natural environment, e.g. air and water pollution , due to manufacturing process is the main factor. So, UK has responsibility to attempt to research how to solve global warming challenge , such as it has many famous scientists who can devote their scientific skills to cooperate to solve global warming challenge with other countries' scientists. Some weather scientists also hypothesized that human may be at the end of the present warming period. If they are right, it would be bad for humanity, as warmer periods have always been associated with better conditions for economic activity. To sum up, scientists believed that global warming will influence human economic activity to be bad.

● Climate technology of global warming success to UK farmers

Climate alarmists were able to convince a large part of the Western public and a majority of Western politicians of the cause of fighting against the global warming. It supposes itself in an instinctive preference for collectivist solutions in economic and social spheres, with negative to disastrous consequences when scientists are applied in practice, so UK government needs to concern global warming challenge, due to it is possible that it will influence UK natural environment weather to be poor to influence many UK farmers' agricultural and vegetable and fruit and rice wheat etc. food growth successfully. What is the global warming influence to cause disease? For example, ecological alarmists and activists (eco-warriors) never admit they are wrong, they long pursued their fear mongering campaign against chlorine. Their success in branding DDT a dangerous substance had a negative impact on the malaria eradication campaign in poorer parts of the world. Alternatives to be have been far less effective and the result has been the resurgence of malaria cases and the manifold increase in malaria -caused deaths to the largest extent in Africa.

Automation technology in manufacturing industry

Nowadays, UK computer and space explore technology had reached the mature stage. It means that UK government ought not need to continue spend much resource to research these two kind technologies. Otherwise, the automatic manufacturing technology, e.g. human intelligence new product. It has need to develop because human intelligence machines will bring beneficial to satisfy human everyday life need, e.g. hospital patients' activities need, if the patent who can not walk easily, but the human intelligence machine can assist the patient walk to anywhere conveniently. So, he/she does not need to sit on wheel chair and apply the human intelligence machine man to help him/her to drive on the intelligence automatic driving vehicle to go to anywhere conveniently.

Otherwise, increased automation in low wage countries, e.g. China, Korea, Africa, Hong Kong etc. which have traditionally manufacturing firms, could use automatic technological manufacturing to bring lose cost advantage and potentially lose their ability of achieving rapid economy growth by shifting workers to factory jobs. So, UK government and businessmen needs to consider automation technology development, i.e. 3D printing manufacturing industry will encourage UK companies to move manufacturing process, closer to gain the biggest advantage from this 3D automation technology development.

A growing concern of premature de-industrialization in energy and developing countries could require new models and a need un-skillful the UK workforce. In the future, the best way toward for UK cities will reduce their exposure to automation is to boost their technological dynamic and attract more UK skilled workers. Automation technology progress can give UK manufacturers' employee benefits, such as long term healthy productivity improvement, raising productivity efficiency and product quality, macroeconomic and microeconomic effects of automation technological change, it's change will be beneficial to UK society, i.e. automation active labor market policies, which could help UK job seekers find jobs from training to incentive to support self-employment to create high technological job employment chance in UK society. So, raising science, technology, engineering and math subjects update skills level are needed to UK any universities, which can be increasingly important in UK society, these factors could complicate the ability of UK high automation technology education to adopt to the UK automation manufacturing technological change. A talent mismatch already exists in UK, with many well UK educated workers can find employment in lower-skilled jobs. To combat this, greater coordination will be needed between the education, training and employment sectors in UK society.

Why are high automatic technology product development models needed to research to UK any manufacturers? UK government and manufacturers need to consider how to achieve high technology product development models. According to Hauser et al. (2006) indicated the high technology (high tech.) development process, is influenced by the innovative process, bringing products on exception value which stimulate product market demand. Innovation provides products the specific basis for which world economies compete with each other on the global market. Able to find new solutions, innovations generate significant changes in existing markets, destroy them, or create new marketing (Hauser et al. 2006). So, UK manufacturers need to concern on any manufacturing high technology product development process because which can influence any new products development to manufacture to sell to any overseas or domestic both markets successfully.

What is high tech. product meaning? Mohr et al. (2010) argues that there are two reasons why it is important to clarify and specific high technology : (1) due to the impact of technologies on the economy, attempts are made to classify economic production and incomes ; (2) due to the impact of high tech. on the environment. Standard marketing strategies are being modified and adopted , therefore, it is necessary to know the products to focus on. Why UK manufacturers need to consider high technological product process. Nowadays, high tech. products are complex, advanced, requiring specific technical knowledge, which is technologically not discontinued and being produced at the companies which have twice as many technical personnel and invest twice as many in scientific research and development than other companies. Moreover, these products are time-sensitive as scientists are continuously searching for new approaches for invention of more advanced technologies which make all preceding ones lower-ranking. The most important, nowadays global consumers will adopt the particular technology. It means that global customers may delay adopting new high-tech. products and in order to mitigate the prolonged uncertainty require a high degree of education and information about the product and need post-purchase reassurance.

Anyway, nowadays customer individual needs in high tech. environments are characterized by sudden changes related to unpredictable fashion. Even, consumers concern about how to preserve new product' competitive technological standard is completely incompatible with technological uncertainty. The most important factor is the prevalence rate of any new products development process, which is influenced by slower than of traditional products. In many cases high-tech. automatic product market are being materialized slower than which are expected. The technological uncertainty challenges will exist in development process, such as uncertainty related to the timetable for development of the question whether the new product will be function as promised. In automatic high-tech. industries, the time requires for product development is difficult to predict as , commonly, it takes longer than expected , uncertainty related to unanticipated consequences and uncertainty about the product life cycle related to competition products. In conclusion, these factors will influence new automatic technology product development process unsuccessful, so UK manufacturers will need to concern on any high technological automatic product's manufacturing process.

Before, all over the world presented picture of demonstrate in London on the occasion of the meeting of the G20. Some economists indicated disastrous economy consequences will occur to any one of Western country , such as UK, so if any one of Western country did not consider automatic technology development to itself country. They indicated one example, such as material incentives to produce disappeared throughout Russia and, when Society leadership called off the experiment, the country faced industrial output reduced to 10% of what had been registered in 1914 and agricultural output reduced to such low levels as to cause widespread famine.

Why would UK encounter disastrous economy consequences if UK government did not encourage manufacturers spend money to invest to innovate automatic technology industry? According to a variety of anthropological studies, a collectivity is unable to operate efficiently with everybody giving talent workers have chance to devote whose best effort to manufacture any high technological products, e.g. human intelligence vehicle or airplane. Hence, economic incentives are needed to UK manufacturers to invest high technological automatic industry development. Because the economists predict UK will have many talent worker numbers, their number will be more than a certain number of normal effort workers, due to UK technological education level is very excellent to provide to train many young technological manufacturing students to find this kind of high technological manufacturing job. So, the high technological manufacturing job seekers will increase and it won't decrease to UK job market in the future.

Assuming that UK high technological automatic manufacturing workers who would desire only to introduce changes in the workings of the international economic order and policies of countries participating in the present economic order rather than change the order itself, what will be UK manufacturers their specific economic preferences in the future? It implies tnat either concentrate on spending more investment to automatic high technological development, e.g. human intelligence automatic high technological products or still concentrate on spending more investment to common traditional technological products.

However, UK was a developed Western country which had had strong automatic high technological development effort very long time. Otherwise, it compared to some developing countries, such as Asian China, Hong Kong, Korea etc. Asian countries their future economic growth rate will show un- surprising , different patterns, so the Asian countries has weak effort to invest high automatic technological product development, such as human intelligence technological development. The catching-up process suggests low economic growth rate in the high automatic technological product development to the Asian developing countries in the future.

Hence, the future economists predict that it views as probable successors of the Western world economic leadership if any Western country , such as UK manufacturers who prefer to invest to any high automatic technological products development , e.g. developing on human intelligence automatic technological products more than traditional common technological products development. On the one side, but it seems important to stress that two very poor countries among the challengers-China and India-are examples of countries that changed their institutions and economic policies from no or little economic freedom to more economic freedom. Because there two countries whose governments prefer to lend loans to encourage their country manufacturers prefer to invest high automatic technological products manufacturing. On the other side, attitudes toward foreign direct investment (FDI) have undergone change since the 1960 s and a large majority of less developed countries, e.g. China and India are now competing strongly among themselves and with developed market economies for direct investment from multinational companies. So, UK will face China and India high automatic technological product competitors in the future. And in fact, all countries that joined Western developed economies did that without much (if any) external inflow of public resources. It is right time that UK government needs to lend loans to encourage domestic manufacturers to invest high automatic technological products to raise whose international high technological products sale effort to win its future competitors. So, machine resources will be increased demand to o UK manufacturers if who chose to spend machine resources to innovate to manufacture any new and high technological automatic products to raise human daily life needs in the future. It means that it is right time UK manufacturers need buy much machines to prepare to manufacture many future high technological automatic products when these machine prices are low. Because the future global machine prices will possible be raised if many China and India manufacturers will also buy many machines in the future. For example, USA government had provided much financial support to assist sugar cane producers to develop their businesses. And they are dependent to a much larger extent than sugar cane producers and sugar processors in the USA on government. Without very high subsidies to renewable energy generation, they would not have survived at all. So, USA government had been the first country which could lent much financial assistance to encourage domestic renewable energy generation manufacturers to develop high technological energy manufacturing business. So, UK government needs follow USA to lend financial assistance to encourage domestic high technological automatic industry development. Future economists also predict China and India will be competitors for future leadership in the global economy, special high technological products. China has been the media and analyst's favorite for quite some time. Quantitative projections have seemingly supported such expectation. Such as China and India had manufactured many high technological new space rockets products, ocean war large ships etc. Moreover, China has become one of the major world trade players in the early twenty-first century.

Many long-term forecasts, assuming similarly high economic growth rates in the decades ahead, predict that China will surpass the USA in terms of aggregate GDP somewhere between 2020 and 2030 or later, say between 2030 and 2050 year. The future economists conclude on the basis of these predictions that China will not only pass the USA in aggregate product

(GDP), but its economy and economic policies will influence the rest of the world to a similar extent that the USA does at present.

I stressed a very important point, namely that the UK future high technological automatic product competitor China and India, namely that economies not only grow, but in the process change their structure. China and India have been industry very rapidly (the first transition) and building the physical infrastructure that accompanies industrialization changes to technology in the future. However, at a certain per capita GNP level the two countries, such as China and India will face another structural shift when which technological development will reach the mature stage in the future. China and India had been primarily historical pattern of economic development because the shift in the role of engine of growth from industry to services is to a much greater extent a qualitative shift. Both higher and different skills are required. And, even more importantly, interactions generating ideas driving the highly human-capital-intensive service economy require a much freer environment, not only in the economic area. Chinese exports have been heavily labor-intensive. This being the case, they contributed to the expansion of industrial employment, offering for the first time in the history of China a taste of (very modest) prosperity to more than 100 million new industrial workers and their families. This is the major component of the success accomplished by Chinese economic growth. Richer trade partners create room for more trade, so the Chinese should hope that intra-South trade, that is, trade between the emerging economies of Asia, the Middle East, Africa and Latin America, will open up new and growing opportunities. I presume that if Western economy , such as UK did not developed high technological automatic industry to stable their social welfare, so thoroughly slowed down their economic growth.

Will it allow China to accomplish the transition to a mature, innovation, service-sector-based market economy? It has allowed the economy to industrialize much more successfully, even if the labor shift from agriculture to industry has not yet been completed. But it is a long way off the next major test: the second high technological industry transition of the economic structure to China. Bear in mind that Russia attempted it twice and failed at both attempts.

But even, assuming that China at some point in the future does succeed in accomplishing the second transition, will it be able to supersede the USA, for example, as the main global high automatic technological innovation center if it wants to become the No.1 global high technological industry economy? Given the nature of the centralized state and its stability to collect financial resources , China's ability to increase research and development expenditure to high automatic technological products and to hire a mass of researchers, engineers, technicians and other specialists should not be doubted. This process in already taking place.

But , again, Soviet Russia already exceed the USA in the R&D/GDP ratio in the 1970s, long before the communist collapse, with no effects on its innovativeness. Inputs matter less than outputs, quantity in the innovation process mean much less than quality. The latter characteristics depends importantly on economic, civic and even political institutions. Otherwise, independent India had three options open to it in 1946s. It could pursue spontaneous economic development, with some state intervention to be sure, along the lines of basically free market capitalism; it could turn the clock back and try to recreate the rural-agricultural and handicraft based. The dominant way of thinking was Society -style priority to industrialization and , within industralization , priority to heavy industry. In other words, not textiles and clothing, which has been developing well in India since the mid- nine teen century, but production of sewing machines and , even better, production of machines the produce sewing machines.

The results were only to be expected. The heavy stress on the expansion of capital-intensive heavy industries in a very poor country quickly strained the ability of the Indian economy to generate adequate savings. Moreover, some of these industries were above the level of industrial competence of an underdeveloped economy. Thus, the amount of required resources (capital, skilled labor) was usually larger per unit of output than in the same industries in more mature, richer industries economies. In another view point, India will develop light industries, just as any other poor country with a great deal of unskilled labor, had a comparative advantage and no less importantly, an economy in which, due to their low capital/labor ratio, light industries could employ many more people, spreading prosperity more widely in a poor country. So, it explain that why China will have more effort to develop heavy high technological industry in the future. Thus, India got less economic efficiency, less employment than in a spontaneously developing economy, less ability to compete internationally in light industries suitable for an underdeveloped economy and finally got heavy industry unable to compete even on the domestic market and, therefore requiring no less heavy a dose of protection. Overall India got an underperforming economy, in particular in its relations with the rest of the world.

To conclude by comparing the performance of the traditional sectors of the Indian economy and the performance of its modern, human -capital-intensive subsector of manufacturing and skill intensive service sector. The latter both employ workers with high-and medium -high skillful level (in branches ranging from computer software and biotechnology and pharmaceutical high technological light industry). India is ahead of China in terms of the output and export of such products and services. Thus, it implies that UK ought concentrate on developing high automatic heavy high technological industry, e.g. human intelligence technological products because these industry is not better development to other many countries' strong effort , such China and India large population countries.

Reference

Hauser, J. Tellis, G. J; Griffin, A. 2006. Research On Innovation: A Review And Agenda For Marketing Science. 25(6): 687-717.

Mohr, G. J. Griffin, A. 2010. Research On Innovation : A Review And Agenda For Marketing Science. 25 (6): 687-717.

US Future Unique Technology

Environment protection technology

Some economists predict developing countries every city in the global 750 is projected to have a larger future technological economy growth. But the diversity of developing countries' economic performance is large. Developing economy cities, such as China, Japan, Hong Kong, Korea cities can grow rapidly by acquiring capital and technological know-how and putting them to use by their rapidly growing urban labor forces. Even, these developing countries cities' rapid technological development can impact to US labor market supply.

Due to future rapid technological development to these developing countries, the result will cause developing countries cities, such as Asia China, Hong Kong, India cities economy growth will rapidly. Otherwise, developed western countries cities, such as US, UK, Canada, Australia, Span, Germany etc. countries lie close to the technological frontier have stable urban populations and more limited investment and job creation opportunities. It will influence these developed countries' economic growth is slow than the developing countries. Due to developing Asia countries cities will prefer to invest more technological development to compare to developed countries, such as US, UK, Canada, Australia, Span, Germany etc. countries. Therefore developed countries, such as US, UK, Canada, Australia, Span, Germany etc. countries tend to grow more slowly. It seems developing Asia countries, such as Hong Kong, China, Korea etc. countries urban and central cities economic performance within developing countries will be better than developed countries, such as UK, US urban and central cities within five years.

Thus, I suppose that future developed countries, such as US the speed of technological development will be slower to compare developing countries, such as Hong Kong , China, Korea, India etc. countries. Then, it will bring this question: How to solve developed countries, such as US, Washington, New York etc. cities future economic slow growth challenge? For future developed country cities, such as New York, Washington etc. large cities' technological investment and location decision, it will need understand that diversity is essential. Various factors can have an impact on US country intra-national urban cities performance, including sector structures, agglomeration benefits, infrastructure quality. For example, US country central government needs have tolerance of diverse performance, land supply and US city governance plan. It aims to raise US central and urban cities' future economic performance. Moreover, US country will need to concern above issues to arrange how to improve central and urban city economic development . Specially, it will need to concern technology innovation to encourage many overseas technology investors to anticipate different kinds of technology products innovation, e.g. human intelligence machine, mobile, computer etc. high technology products. It aims to absorb different countries' new technological knowledge of different kinds of high technological products to excite US domestic or foreign countries consumers' desires to choose to buy many different kinds of high technological products to raise US GDP growth in US technological product sector industry in the future.

Agricultural development technology

Some economists indicate that there are five trends reshape to impact rural America' future economy. They include that digital economy will shift future America rural economy. US quality of life will change a lot, the US rural economy will stay uneven, US commodities will compete in global markets and will give less benefit to US rural economy and US new products will revolutionize US agriculture economy.

The first aspect impacts to US agriculture economy, the US future rural economy stays uneven. Growth will concentrate in 4 out of 10 rural places and they have scenery, a retail hub, or one next to a city in US. The impact on rural America includes some rural places will try to manage growth , but many places on a quest for new economic engines. Thus, it will bring these questions to US rural economy impact, such as : Who will be US businessmen clients? The struggling farmers? The struggling farm-dependent country? The booming mountain area? The rural area transforming into city?

The second aspect impacts to US agriculture economy, due to US commodities will compete in global markets if it will bring a smaller benefit in US rural economy. Then, US farm scale will cut costs and competition fewer US farms and places will depend on farm income. What is the impact of commoditization on rural America? There are more farms depend on area jobs and it creates a new imperative to add value. What is the impact of commodity on US clients? The need for competitive commodities remains, but the payoff for added value is rising and community impacts are important.

The third aspect impact to US agriculture economy, new products will revolutionize agriculture. Major, shift from commodities to products, spurred by biotech, means two agriculture in the future and two rural America . Hence, US future agriculture determination the rural economy will be declined. A future new US agriculture supply chain integrator will be caused from the traditional farming supply chain procedure the change to outsourced contractor farming supply chain procedure, such as: In beginning, from farmer will outsource supply chain contract to processor, then contract to distributor and contract to food retailer final step.

The fourth aspect impacts to US agriculture economy, what will be two agricultures impact to the US future economy? The first US agriculture impact will be US commodity agriculture. It focuses on production capabilities, farming foods production will be thin margins maintained with technology and big sale. The second US agriculture impact will be product agriculture. It focuses on consumer needs, farming foods production margins will be protected by capturing value and building business relationship. Thus, it will bring these questions concern what the impact of product agriculture which can influence to US economy. How to apply biotechnological agricultural techniques and farming product application to raise US farming productivity? How to build world class agricultural (farm) producing chains that benefit to US farming produces production method?

How can US faming foods producers participation or lead in product chains?

In the fifth aspect impacts to US agricultural economy, it is digital economy impacts US rural agriculture. Future diversity economic base can encourage US farming product agriculture to enter rural digital agricultural service consumption sector to change US agricultural consumer individual shopping habit. What will impact to US farmers? Digital agricultural economy will bring these questions: Who will lead in broadband digital agricultural technology? How to launch e-markets and businesses and how to cooperate with US rural farmers? What will impact on US agricultural on natural resource management aspect and on how to US commodity to build amenity strategies? However, rural America's future will be shaped by policies that will encourage agricultural technology adoption, it will enhance farming worker skills, it will improve rural quality of life and it will ensure access to capital to bring US agricultural economy growth.

High level education and high birth
rate population raising technology

According to John G. (2016) indicated that " a point forecast is that GDP per capita will rise well under 1% per year in the longer run, with overall GDP growth of a little over 1 to 12%. The main drivers of slow growth are educational attainment and demographics. First, rising educational attainment will add less to productivity growth than it did historically. Second because of the aging and retirement of baby boomers, employment will rise more slowly than population which in turn, is projected to rise slowly relative to history." Thus, it seems that some economists believe education and born rate will influence future US employment method. They assume that the employment and growth ratio will rise and unemployment ratio will deadline of US will increase birth ratio and future there are many young people (students) can have chance to accept high education degree to raise whose education level to prepare to enter different kinds of high educational jobs market to work in the future.

Considering a more growth accounting perceptive on productivity growth. According to the analysis in Fernald (2015) which uses a multi-sector growth model for the projections. It indicated that although, the details differ and if bases projections on TFP data since 2004, it also implies a preferred point estimate of 1.6% per year in US over this short period. The " fundamentals" of labor-productivity growth (namely, growth in total factor productivity , TFP) have exceeded the actual realization for reasons that reflect the unwinding of dynamic of labor quality and capital depending associated with the great recession. Thus, how to raise labor quality which concerns how to raise educational level to young people in any country will be one labor economic challenge in US in the future.

Fernald (2015) also explained " the shortfall" in productivity growth relative to fundamentals reflects, at least in part, the unwinding of two dynamics associated with the great recession. He indicated that first, at the end of the great recession business had a lot of capital relative to labor, which has attended the need of add capacity to meet demand in recent years. In contrast to the outsized growth in capital deepening from 2007 to 2010 year, we have seen capital "shallowing" since 2010 year. Second, businesses fired low-skilled workers during the recession, which raised labor quality in 2007 year to 2010 year period. As these potential workers have been rehired, the growth rate of labor quality has added less.

Thus, on the one hand, when one country encounters economic recession, many employers will like to employ high educational level and high skilled labor to raise productivity. If US encountered economic recession, but it had none (lacked) enough high educational level and high skilled knowledgeable workers to be supplied to the labor market in US. Then, US will encounter long term economic recession period, it can't shorten economic recession period. Thus, US will need to let many US young people have effort to study to prepare enough high educational level knowledge to do different kinds of professional or high knowledgeable or high technological jobs in future US labor market.

However, US high knowledgeable labor can also assist US businessmen to raise productivity growth. Due to labor quality could be grown by high educational and increasing number of knowledgeable workers. On the other hand, moreover, if there are many US young married parents who will either choose not born any babies for next generation or choose born only one to four children. Then, future US will have a small numbers of young people to be supplied to primary schools, high schools, even universities to study. It also means the university level graduate student numbers will decrease also. So, low birth rate factor can also influence the high knowledgeable labor numbers to be supplied to future US labor market. So, I recommend that US government needs to encourage many young parents choose born next generation and provides student loans to lend to poor families to support whose children can have more chance to attempt to go to high schools or universities to study in the future.

Artificial Intelligent Socio-economic development technology

US development practitioners are increasingly aware of the role that US social and political structures play in future shaping US's development paths and results. In this context, US macro social analysis needs to understand the ways in which power relations act to circumscribe the opportunities available to poor US people to improve their situation. For example, US donor organizations need to understand of relevant US social structures, such as informal institutions or other relevant US social practices in US.

This provides an entry point for understanding the broader US political environment or challenges in a particular sector or process. Furthermore, any US donor organizations need to place greater emphasis on the analysis of livelihoods and economic opportunities and their relationship to reduce the unequal of gap between rich and poor US citizen in US societies . Thus, US government needs to encourage donor organization participants choose to do the reasonable donor behavioral to aim to reduce the unfair donor spending to the unneeded donor assistance beneficiaries. To let us socio-economic has more balance chance to every US poor citizen in US society. So, it can also raise average every US poor citizen feels better quality of life in US society.

How does the rise of US exports to East Asia factor influence US economy change? Export have become an increasing important source of revenue for both national and regional forms in the United States. How does the primary growth market for US exports to influence US economy growth? I recommend the developing nations in East Asia will the developing nations in East Asia will soon rival today's industrial nations as the most important US trading partner . In view of the rapid growth of US exports and their geographic shift toward developing nations.

Some economists indicates that two tends in recent US export performance are particularly notable. First, US exports have increased rapidly relative to total US output, development with important implications for the entire economy. Approximately 130,000 US firms employing over 10 million domestic workers, export their products (US Bureau of the census,1993). Second, the geographic distribution of US exports has been shifting dramatically. The industrialized nations of the organization for economic cooperation and development (OCED) account for about 57% of all US exports . However, in recent years of the start of US exports to major trading partners in East Asia. America has been rising and now accounts for 26% of the total. Thus, economic policymakers can no longer make trade related decisions without considering their effect on US exports to East Asia market.

From 1981 to 1987 year, two factors temporarily stemmed the rising tide of 1980 year. First, the US dollar began to appreciate significantly in 1981 year as the United States enacted a restrictive monetary policy and an expansion fiscal policy. From 1981 to 1985 years, the dollar rose almost 50%, thus making US exports more expensive relative to foreign products (Hakki & Whittakersand J, Gregg Whittaker, 1985. " The US dollar recent developments, outlook, and policy options". Federal reserve bank of Kansas city, economic review, Sept./Oct., pp.3-15.) Thus, future US will need to make good international export and import trade relationship with Asia countries, e.g. China, Hong Kong, Japan etc . countries to raise GDP income.

Distance learning education technology

In the past, there fundamental forces have shaped US work labor market, includes an increase in the returns to education. General education upgrading and the large numbers of female need to work. How educational attainment, demographics and human capital will be predicted to influence US future labor market. Some economists believe education is useful to influence US future labor market. They indicate the social returns to education policies today depend on the relative prices that labor of different educational levels will command in future US labor market; current US labor market trends appear to leave a large group behind; less educated males. The rationale for social policies target specifically to this population is strengthened if predicted future outcomes in US labor market will lead this less educated male group numbers to fall down.

How to supply educational level components to influence future changes in US labor supplied? It can change in the size of the US working age population, it can change in hours worked conditional on being of working age, and it can change in the skills (effective human capital units) to US workers of different education levels, gender and age . In US , the labor is supplied by both highly educated men and women increased substantially relative to the supply of labor by the less educated. Among US males this is largely , due to an increase in educational attainment; highly educated US males did not differentially increase their supplied compared to less educated males nor did their experience differential increases in their human capital policy in US. For US females, some economists found large increases in the labor supplied by US working age women that are due to both large increases in hours worked and increase in educational attainment. So, I assume that future US will have many high educational level female labors to work in US society.

Today, human history is at the beginning of a growth industrial revolution. Developments in genetics, artificial intelligence, robotics, nanotechnology, 3D printing and biotechnology will be popular to influence US future job market change. For example, smart systems, product-homes, factories, farms or cities with help to solve problems ranging from supply chain management to climate change. The rise of the sharing economy will allow US human to monetize everything from their empty house to their car.

Due to the future patterns of consumption will change to trend high technology life enjoyment, it will cause production and employment will also change to employ high technological production labor. As entire industries adjust, most US occupations are changed to high technological manufacturing industries. When some US jobs are threatened by others grow through a change in the skill sets required to do them. a key element in understanding how the benefits and burdens of the growth.

Nowadays, the current technological changes of humans and machines , but rather an opportunity for work to truly become a channel though which human recognize full potential. As US is a high technological developed country. I assume many US employers will choose to act to be the first high technological and invention manufacturing leader to encourage which labors need to learn high technological production methods to prepare manufacture any new technological products to sell in the future US domestic or foreign both markets. Thus, it is possible that future high technological manufacturing labor numbers will be shared large go e.g. 50 to 60% future total US labor market.

How can future US labor market affect job creation and productivity growth? US future economic growth requires factor reallocation across US firms and continuous replacement of technologies. US labor market influences US economy dynamism by their impact on the supply of a key factor, skilled workers to US new and expanding firms, US growth -favoring labor market includes portable pension plans and health insurance united to the current US employers, individualized wage-setting and US public income insurance systems that encourage mobility and risk taking.

US future economic growth arises as production shifts from less to more successful firms though the reallocation of factors of production . US labor market can advance restructuring. Overly regulations tend to create a system in which a large share of economic activity occurs in US small firms without the ability to grow. US labor market should be organized to promote potential high growth US firms, especially through decentralized and individualized wage setting, portable jobs.

In the future, US will have many key importance of high growth firms. US capitalism entails a process of creative destination. New ideas continuously challenges act structures, giving rise to structural transformation as successful innovations and new products firms and industries will arise and obsolete ones will decline in US society.

Martin , J. P. (2012) studies pointed to high-growth forms (sometimes known as gazelles) as the main drivers of this process. In the US , an estimated 1% of firms creation 40% of all new jobs and 5% create almost 70% of new jobs. A review of the studies of US firms growth reveals some common findings . US high-growth firms are crucial to net job growth, generating a large share of all net jobs . This is particularly pronounced in recessions, when US high-growth firms continue to grow when other US firms deadline. US small firms are over-represented among high-growth firms, but these US firms come in all sizes . A small subgroup of large high growth firms are major job creators. Such as US high -growth firms are younger on average, US young and small high high-growth firms grows, not through mergers and acquisition and make a larger contribution to net employment growth than do US larger and older higher growth firms, high growth firms are present in all industries. Through they are slightly overrepresented in service industries in US.

Some economists predict that future US will be a flexible labor market, the marginal product of labor and the average wage in an industry should tend toward equally across US firms. Taking advantage of a legislative change to raise cost to US employers a study measured the gap between the marginal product of labor and the average wage in an industry before and after the reform. The gap increased after the legislation, which suggests that the legislation reduced allocative efficiency. Their studies have suggested that total factor productivity could increase by as much as 30% in China and India of they were to attain the US level of allocative efficiency across firms within individual industries. The result implies that plants with low total factor productivity are too large and plant with high total factor productivity are too small relative to the US benchmark of allocative efficiency.

What is allocative efficiency meaning? It occurs when the mix of product produced matches consumer preferences (where marginal benefit equals marginal cost). There products and services are the most profitable, thereby promoting economic growth other research also indicate a strong quantitative effects of strict employment protection legislation on the rate of reallocation in US industries experiments. By relaxing employment protection rules to US developed countries, such as UK, UK etc. with the strictest legislation could increases their reallocation rate by an estimated 50% in the most dynamic sectors, those that benefit most from flexibility.

The effect appears to be particularly strong on the entry-exist margin, which is arguably, especially importation for creative destruction. In future US, if manufacturing industry can have high technological production method to achieve reallocation rate to efficiency to every manufacturing industry. It can have benefit to economic growth, due manufacturing process can be move efficient to avoid cost. Also high technological manufacturing reallocation rate innovation method can influence the future US number of jobs lost in contracting or existing US firms as well as the number of jobs gained in new or expanding US firms in future a certain period divided by the average number of existing jobs. So, US high technological manufacturing reallocation rate innovation method will bring disadvantages to cause many contracting or existing firms job lost, but it will also increase the number of jobs gained in new or expanding firms in US. Thus, if future US manufacturing industry can have high technological reallocation rate innovated successfully. It will raise many new job chances in new or expanding firms in US, but it also have chance to cause many contracting or existing firms job lost or the same time.

What will expected to impact of future computerization on US labor market outcomes? Some economists estimated, about 47% of total US employment is at risk, due to that US wages and educational attainment will exhibit a strong negative relationship with an occupation's probability of computerization. They indicated that the poor performance of global labor markets across advanced economies has intensified the debate about technological unemployment among economists more recently. Indeed, over the past, decades, computers have substituted for a number of jobs, including the functions of bookkeepers, cashier and telephone operators (Bresnahan, 1999, MGI, 2013).

Although the extent of these developments remains to be seen, estimates by MGI (2013) suggests that sophisticated algorithms could substitute for approximately 140 million full time knowledge workers world wise. Hence, when technological process throughout economic history has largely been confined to the machine of manual tasks, requiring physical labor, technological progress in the twenty-first century can be expected to contribute to a wide range of cognitive tasks, which until have largely remained a human domain. Of course, may occupations being affected by these developments act still far from fully computerization, meaning that the computerization of some tasks will simply free-up time for human labor to perform other tasks. Nonetheless, the trend is clear: computers increasingly challenge human labor in a wide range cognitive tasks (Brynjolfsson and Mc Afee, 2011).

Thus, it seems that future US computerization job trend will influence some US traditional labor hand made manufacturing industry to divide some part job duty to let computerization work. However, it will not cause many US manufacturing labor to be dismissed. It can still keep some US manufacturing labors to US employers' needs in the future.

Popular science, technology , engineering
and mathematics
Science, technology , engineering and mathematics workers will drive US innovation and competitiveness by new ideas, new companies and new industries in US. However, US employers frequently concern the supply and availability of this kind of workers. Over the past 10 years, growth in this kind of jobs was three times as fast as growth to general jobs in US. This kind of US workers are also less likely to experience joblessness than other kinds of workers. In the future, science, technology, engineering and mathematics workers will play a key role to grow and raise stability of the US economy.

Bureau of labor statistics, ESA calculation 2010 and 2018 year. indicated these kinds of technology, science and engineering workers had been increasing 7.9% from 2000 to 2010 year growth as well as these kinds of workers had been increasing 17% from 2008 to 2018 year growth. Otherwise, other kinds of workers had been increasing 2.6% from 2000 to 2020 year growth as well as these kinds of workers had been increasing 9.8% from 2008 to 2018 year growth. Hence, these kinds of science, technology and engineering workers increasing rate and increasing level are more than other kinds of workers both twenty years.

The other occupations include positions, such as educators, managers, technicians, health-care professionals or social scientists. The science occupation divides four categories: computer and mathematics, engineering and surveying, physical and life science four categories. The reasons why these kinds of jobs will be trend popularly. We define these kinds of degree holders as persons whose primary or secondary undergraduate major was in a science, engineering or technological field. To using similar logic to what we used in our occupation selection, we exclude business, healthcare, and social science majors.

The US department of commerce, economics and statistics administration analysis showed that a science, technology, engineering and math. (STEM) degree is the typical path to a job related to those kinds of degrees or more than two-thirds of the 4.7 million (STEM) workers with a college degree has an undergraduate (STEM) degree. However, this does not necessarily mean that (STEM) field or their jobs . For example, only 35 per cent of college educated computer and mathematic workers have a degree in computer science or math. Thus, these past data explained that it is possible US science, technology ,engineering and mathematics employers will increase needs and why many US students choose to study these subjects in US. Thus, future US economic growth will depend on developing these kinds of science, technology ,engineering and mathematics industries.

Genetics, human intelligence,
robotics, nanotechnology, 3D
printing and biotechnology
technological industry

In US future, these kinds of jobs will be needed to increase development in genetics, human intelligence, robotics, nanotechnology, 3D printing and biotechnology. For example, smart systems homes, factories, farms grids or cities will help tackle problems ranging from supply chain management to climate change. The rise of US economy growth will allow US people to monetize everything from their empty house to their car in US. These new technological products development will change US patterns of consumption, production and employment adaption are also be changed by US corporations, US government and individuals.

Why will the technological revolution be broader socio-economic, geopolitical and demographic drivers of change to influence future US social economic and consumption pattern change? Future US most occupations will also be changed. When some traditional old jobs are threatened by redundancy and other new technological jobs will grow rapidly, existing jobs are also changed in the skill sets required to do them. The debate is between some economists foresee limitless new job opportunities and foresee massive dislocation of US jobs. In fact, the reality is highly specific to future US high technological production industry, region and high technological occupation in question as well as how US production workers can be raised themselves ability to actions the upgrade level of high technological production ability from various stakeholders to manage high technological production method change.

Overall, this is a modestly positive outlook of US high technological production employment across future most high technological production industries with jobs growth expected in several sectors. However, it is also clear that this need for more talent in certain job categories is accompanied by high skills instability across all job categories. Combined together, future US net job growth and skills instability result in most US businesses with face major recruitment challenges and talent shortages, a pattern already evident in the result and set to get worse over next five years in possible.

The question is how US businesses, government and individuals will react to these new technological job changes, due to talent shortage, mass unemployment and growing inequality challenges will encounter in future US society.

The current technological revolution does not need become a race between humans and machines , but rather an opportunity for work to truly become a channel through which US people recognize their potential. So, if US traditional low manufacturing skillful workers lack talent to learn new skills to prepare to do future new technological manufacturing jobs, such as 3 D printing, robotics, nanotechnology, biotechnological high technological products manufacturing jobs. Then, it will cause increasing of unemployment rate to some not talent US low manufacturing skillful workers. So, US government or high technological product industry employers need to consider this future unemployment challenge will be caused by high technological products manufacturing changing influences. It seems high technological development will cause these low manufacturing skillful workers unemployed rising numbers as well as high manufacturing skillful workers human capital shortage global challenges will exist.

In the future, the driver of changes to influence US demographic and socio-economic growth. They may include: changing work environments and flexible working arrangements. It means new technologies are enabling workplace innovations , such as remote working, co-working spaces and teleconferencing. Rising of the middle class in Asia markets. It means the world's economic center is shifting towards the Asia developing countries. Some economists predict that Asia will be projected to account for 66% of the global middle class and for 59% of middle class consumption by 2030 year. In addition, climate change, natural resource will be constraints to a greener economy. It means that climate change is a major driver of innovation as organizations search for measures to help adjust to its effects. As global economic growth consumers are needed to lead to demand for natural resources and raw materials, over explanation implies higher extraction most and degradation ecosystem and these challenges will also impact US employment changes needs. All US government also needs to concern future global economic change influence.

US entrepreneurship innovation

Some economists believed the interplay between entrepreneur , innovation and economic geography growth in the United states of America have close relationship . Because future innovation is the driving force of growth in the knowledge economy to US . They assumed that if future US entrepreneurships chose to act as new firm formation, which will prefer to accept any new technological innovation to manufacture any new technological products and reallocate any new resources to apply to concentrate on manufacturing any new technological products within firms. For example, Bernard, et al. (2006) find that one third of the net increase in real U.S. manufacturing output between 1972 and 1997 is due to the net adding and dropping of products by surviving firms, a contribution that dwarfs that of net firm entry and exist. Clearly new firm formation is only one dimension of innovation and existing firms account for a large share of total research and development (R&D), in many industries such as pharmaceuticals. It seems US any industries will need spin off of existing operations and the acquisition of independent start-ups are now important dimensions of new process and product development. Thus, innovation is an important factor to influence US economic growth in the future.

However, it will have challenges to US different industries when the causal connections between entrepreneurship, innovation and growth arises. For example, US employment growth of large, middle and small sizes of entrepreneurships will be strongly positively correlated with US any new firms formation, but this doesn't necessarily imply that entrepreneurship causes growth . There may be one factor that causes US employment growth and US firms formation to co-vary, and it is hard to find instructions that affect US firm formation, but have no independent effect on US employment growth.

The interpretation of the correlation between US employment growth and US firm formation relates to old debates in US economic geography about whether US workers follow US firms, or US firms follow workers or there are mutually reinforcing feedbacks between US firms' and workers' locations decisions. So, some economists believed that, US any domestic geography economic growth will possible be caused by these factor , such as either US geography firms innovation factor or US geography high technological workers high level productivity factor or US geography firms innovation or US geography high technological workers high level productivity both combining factor. But the challenge will cause, it assumes that future many US entrepreneurships choose to innovate to manufacture whose products. Although, many high technological manufacturing workers employment chance will be raised, but it also cause many low technological manufacturing workers employment chance will be reduced as the same time. So, it is difficult to keep high technological and low technological both workers who have same fair employment chance as the same time in the future US society if US planned to achieve the future knowledgeable innovation economic society.

However, to achieve this innovation dream, the economists give opinions to US government which will need to encourage the foundations of US entrepreneurial policy and distinguish four broad actors: (a) individual agents who identify business opportunities and choose to exploit them. (b) new formed businesses which innovate using new knowledge and other resources, (C) the economy including all institutions that influence economic growth, and (d) US society is as the collection of all agents who are the ultimate beneficiaries of wealth creation. Within this organizing framework, US entrepreneurships will be easily shaped or changes the overall business climate to achieve knowledge economic society in the future.

Intangible assets ecommerce technology

What are the four big factors of intangible assets? Some economists indicated they include knowledgeable capital, human capital, social capital and entrepreneurs capital. Nowadays, globalization and increased competition will cause new types of pressure to influence US economic growth. So, US companies need have flexibility, the ability to immediately adapt to market developments, and pro-activism in creating future markets. The relative importance of physical growth: However, soft production factors, that is those related to personal knowledge are becoming more important to influence US future economic growth, which regards to human capital and knowledge as driving factor of economic growth in industries developed countries, such as US.

All these soft production factors can be grouped in what is known intangible assets. These assets can be defined as non-material factors that contribute to enterprise performance in the production of products or the provision of services, or that are expected to generate future economic benefits to the entities or individuals that control their deployment (Akerlof & Kranton , 2000).

Whether it has a close relationship between these intangible assets and US regional economic growth? Some economists had researched to have more reliable quantitative statistical information to do report in above four big factors how to effect on US regional economical growth influence. Their report indicated that returns from human and social capital are taken as homogeneous for US all regions. They also indicated these two sets of questions in their report. The first one, dealing with knowledge accumulation, addresses, among others the following issues:

(a) How does innovation and knowledge accumulation occur within firms and hoe does it impact on economic performance?

(b) What is the role of universities in regional, national and global knowledge accumulation processes?

The second set of questions addresses the key knowledge diffuses over space and how this diffusion impacts on economic performances.

In particular:

(c) To what extent knowledge diffusion is conditioned by spatial proximity?

(d) What is the impact of knowledge accumulation and diffusion on economic performance?

They indicated to answer these questions, having reliable measures of how innovation process occurs, of the actors that take part in it and the mechanisms that are in place is important. They pointed out that the systemic nature of US regional intangible asset demands indicators that grasp two kinds of capabilities: network capabilities , i.e. connectivity, both intra-and-inter-regional and organizational capabilities, as well as their dynamic in US. These indicators have been applied to the study of linkages and relationships between US firms and between US firms and US universities, highlighting the mechanisms through which those actors contribute to the processes of knowledge accumulation, generation and diffusion.

They also found results: How does knowledge accumulation occur within US firms and how does it impact on US economic performance? They included collaborations with competitors are most commonly undertaken at early stages of the development projects, those with buyers and suppliers are more likely to result in the introduction of new products and processes: At the same, it has been highlighted that, regardless of the industry, the most innovative firms, i.e. those more able to absorb knowledge are more likely to participate in collaborative networks.

Thus, US future entrepreneurships need to offer knowledge accumulation opportunities for US regional firms and research institutions to benefit and contribute to global network of US expects to achieve rapid regional economic growth. US's entrepreneurships also needs to explore organizational innovation, those US firms whose structure enables learning by doing, using and interacting by relying, among other things on parallel development teams. Semi-autonomous work teams and reduced management layers are more likely to introduce new products to the future US domestic and foreign both markets.

What is the role of US universities in US regional, national and global knowledge accumulation processes? US universities can heavily influence US regional, national and global knowledge accumulation processes. For instance, when collaborating with multi-national enterprises, they may affect simultaneously the three level. Their report had highlighted interesting results on the local impact of universities: when it has been found that top ranked departments are significantly associated with partnerships involving spatially close industry partners, it has also emerge geographical proximity, is nt the main driver of collaboration choices. These are found to depend largely on US firms' networks and universities' specific characteristics. Among other things, the cultural traditional of academic institution has been shown to influence the ability to collaborate with industry and commerce research.

Networks characteristics have emerged as crucial in determining academic knowledge transfer: the better the access to international networks, the higher the patenting activity, have the knowledge transfer to US industry. This implies that the set of tools of knowledge based economic development should include not only research and development, but also clever ways of supporting academic research network.

To conclude, if US expected research development can assist economic growth. Then, US academics universities and companies both need to co-operate to carrying on experimenting any kinds of research and prepare to assist any US product innovation more easily. So, the intangible asset, not as scientists, technology, US universities' and firms' research fund which is an conditional factor to influence US regional research and development economic growth in the future.

Ecommerce social economic development technology

Has it relationship between social influence and economic environment in future US? For example, the social factors that are positively correlated with the economic growth (i.e. the expected years of schooling and the life expectancy) and respectively, the factors that are negatively correlated with US future economic growth (i.e. the US population or risk of poverty and the unemployment rate).

The improvement of the US future economic environment will be an objective of the macroeconomic policy on short, medium and also long term. The importance of social factors upon US future economic growth, considering that the future used macroeconomic indicator, GDP per capita, is not most proper measure for the future US nation welfare. Due to GDP per capital fails to take into consideration some specific sectors of the US social economy, such as the black market.

Until recently, some economists rely on culture is as a possible determinant of economic phenomena. However, in current years, better techniques and more date made it possible to identify systematic differences in people's preferences and beliefs and to relate them to various measures of cultural environment suggest an approach to introduce cultural-based explanation that can be tested and are able to substantially understand economic phenomena.

The increased importance of social factors relies on a basic concept. Some theory is measured to economic growth which has wrong assumption. For example, the fiscal and monetary policies focused on increasing the national income, which lead consequently to economic growth. The reason most of economic opinions have been argued because whose opinions are based on a wrong hypothesis, according to which the nation welfare is based only on the level of income.

Can social factors influence US future economic growth? Human development history, global life expectancy has been experiencing these stages: from the industrialization process, the technologic progress, the medical evolution, the scientific research, these stages were also related to internal causes, specific to some developed countries, e.g. US developed country. Thus, the differences are significant and are linked both to US life expectancy level and the GDP /capita. Such as US population is less than China population too much. Although, US land area is near to China area. It seems US will encounter life expectancy level need to prepare its technological development to raise economy growth of opportunity. For example, Africa and Asia are still facing major economic and social issues. The access to a health life and medical services are still long terms objectives for countries with low life expectancy.

According to Harrison & Huntington (2000), the analysis of social factors helps understanding the human behavior with respect to consumption, savings, investment system, expectations and attitudes towards the economic circumstances, which also have a major impact on the economic growth. The evolutions of economic and social environment are needed for US future development. In order to eliminate the gap of living standard, outside resources and support US needs have good social indicators study plan to concern econometric model to rise poor people living standard in future US society between rich and poor people who are living in US. However, I believe the social factors include demographic and culture, population's structure factors which are one important social indicator to influence the distribution of the US social public income.

Barro & Sala-i-Martin (1996) defined culture is as the sum of symbols, meanings, habits values, behaviors and social artifacts which characterize a distinctive and specific human population group. For decades, economists and social thinkers debated the influence of population change on economic growth. Bloom et. al (2001) defined three alternative hypotheses: that population growth restrict, promotes or is independent of economic growth . Each hypothesis was sustained with strong arguments, and all the arguments mostly focused on population size and growth. The debates revealed other important issues, such as the age structure of the population, the way in which the population is distributed across different age groups.

The economists indicated that people's economic behavior varies at different stages of life, changes in a country's age structure can have significant effects on its economic performance. So, such as US, if it had a high proportion of children are likely to devote a high proportion of resources to their care, which would tend to depress the pace of economic growth. By contrast, if US's population falls within the working wages, the added productivity of this group can produce an increase in the economic growth. This is how the combined effect of this large working age population and health, family, labor, financial and human capital policies can create cycles of wealth creation. On the other hand, if US a large proportion consists of the elderly , the effects can be similar to those of a very young population; a large share of resources is needed by a relatively less productive segment of the population , which likewise can inhibit economic growth in future US society.

Further Bloom et al. (2001) analyzed the three main mechanisms of population's structure for determining economic growth (labor supply, savings and human capital) and their dependence of policy environment. They indicated that a growing number of adults will only be productive of there is sufficient flexibility in the labor market to allow its expansion, and macroeconomic policies that permit and encourage investment, people will only save if who have access to adequate saving mechanisms and have confidence in domestic financial markets and the demographic transition creates conditions where people will tend to invest in their health and education, offering great economic benefits, special in the modern world's increasing sophisticated economies.

It seems future US labor market will need a growing number of adults to supply , a stable domestic financial market to encourage US people have more confidence to save money in banks, a stable health and education sector industry can encourage US people have confidence to invest to do this kind of health and education service industry. Instead of population of working age factor will influence US economic growth. However, US people living culture will also influence US economic growth. For example, if it has a trend that there are many US young people like often go to shopping in relax time, because who feel shopping is their young group entertainment in the year. Then, the year US GDP growth will be possible raised, due to there are many US young people prefer to spend for shopping expenditure suddenly in the year. In conclude, in social environment of cultural and population of working age size will influence US future economic growth.

Online tourism technology

Today, US online tourism sale industry has always been one of America's great home growth industries. Today, more than 8 million Americans are employed in travel and tourism. For example, US domestic South Carolina, hospitality and tourism has been as the largest local industry, providing tens of thousands of families directly or indirectly with jobs. Predicting global tourism consumption needs work be increased. US will experience in a changing economy, tourism industry will provide job security to many Americans as well as the service -oriented nature of many travel positions and these jobs are difficult, if it is impossible to outsource.

Many people accept to buy air tickets from online sale channel. Will future America government play an important role to influence future US online air ticket tourism sale method to raise online travel consumption behavior? However, some have questioned in recent years whether US policies have harmed the ability of the tourism industry to expand. One of the most frequently discussed concerns involves American visa policy, when European Union allows tourists from 26 European countries and almost all of the America and Australia to visit without a visa. America policies require some travelers from friendly countries, such as Brazil, to travel thousands of miles from home to attend the in-person interview needed to secure a tourist visa. Although, the US White House has taken steps to reduce rise wait times in recent years, in some parts of the world, like Vietnam and Turkey, the US tourist visa application process can be a multi-month process (US Travel Association , 2014).

Will the visa waiver program impact driving increases in US impact driving increases in US tourist volumes? Some economist analysis found that when a typical country joins the visa waiver program, it sees a notable increase in the number of countries who chose to visit the US in the immediate years. That follow over the course of its first five years in the US visa wavier program, the number of tourists arriving from a participating country rises by 16.4%. Also their analysis indicated to expand the visa waiver program to some countries would result in $7.66 billion in additional tourist spending within a five year period. It would also create at least 50,000 American tourism jobs within 5 years. Purchases of products and services by visitors contribute foreign significantly to job creation and economic growth in US international travelers to US purchased more than $180 billion amount . In addition, tourism generates a trade surplus as foreign visitors spend more in the US. So, US enjoyed a $57 billion trade maintained a trade surplus in tourism every year. Some economists indicated that India is likely to contribute to the growth in foreign travel to the US . If India government can ensure which have enough numbers of foreign travelers are encouraged to choose to travel to US. In the future, India will be one important tourism cooperation partner to US. So, US ought achieve online travel sale strategy to promote to Indian to know what online travel advantages can give to them in the future, e.g. reducing time to buy air ticket, convenience, cheap e-ticket price, avoiding to lose air seat supply, more airlines choice providing. These are online e-ticket sale attractive characteristics to India online e-ticket sale market. Thus, US ought concentrate on promoting this kind of online travel sale service to India in order to raise US many airline e-tickets sale numbers.

Nowadays, China and India population growth rate are rapidly. Population growth can have several disadvantage effects on the economic expansion and performance to China and India. Does it influence cultural and sociological links between the following per capita income, rates, technological advancement , education aspects? China with 1.32 billion people and India with 1.1 billion people. Though, they each enjoy a large labor force advantage, several key economic factors have contributed to how the Chinese and Indian populations have grown and what differing effects that growth has had on their developing economies. Although, there two countries have high population growth rates, but the poor people has low standard of living.

So, when these two countries population sizes are large, but the standard of living will be low, and population will be reduced by either the preventive check (international reduction of fertility) or by the positive check (malnutrition, disease, and famine). It seems china and India governments think overpopulation challenge will cause social crime increasing, education competition, raising the job applicants number will increase, but the jobs supply number won't increase faster than job applicants number, and it will cause unemployment etc. social challenge in the future long term. So, why China and India governments will choose to control birth rates every year. However, in these developing countries, children are often as an economic asset, a tool to help increase agricultural production. Demand or need for large number of children is driven down by improvements in living standards and child survival and by the modern of economies. The movement away from agricultural production and into more modern industries in the manufacturing and services sectors need the necessity to have numbers of children to prepare to supply to China and India future manufacturing and services job markets.

However, US is a developed countries. The country main GDP growth source is high technological industry. Hence future children birth rate is not necessary to prepare to supply for manufacturing or service industries needs mainly. It seems US population birth rate is stable. So, overpopulation challenge won't be caused easily. Can population growth influence US economic growth? US is different to China and India. US's population growth rate is less. Hence, if US population growth rate can rise. It won't have overpopulation challenge. US needs have many young people number who can have high technological knowledge to prepare to have enough supply to do the future high technological different kinds of positions to build social economic growth in the future. Hence, US ought encourage young people choose to marry and to born next generation children to supply future different kinds of high technological jobs of needs to raise technological productivity and they (high technological manufacturing workers) will be the main production of factor to influence future US economic growth in the high technological manufacturing sector.

Thus, I believe the effect future US of population growth will influence US future economic growth as the same time. Also, it is the right time, US government needs to assist universities have enough afford resources, e.g. university fund, technological educational courses, lectures etc. to provide future US technological education students' needs in the future. So, it brings this question: What can determine US economic growth?

In global macro-economic influence, since 1973 year, per captia income growth in the US and other advanced countries has slowed to 2.2 % a year or almost half the 3.9% annual rate of the preceding quarter century . If the US had maintained the level of growth experiences in the 1950 year and 1960 year, real per capita income today would be about 71% greater than it actually is. In contrast, it has been estimated that eliminating the variability in US consumption since world war II would be equivalent to boosting current real consumption by only about 4.8%. If the choice is between long-term growth policies and further short-term stabilization policies long term clearly have the potential for higher benefits. Hence, what factors determine US economic growth (David M & Roy J, 1993).

According to traditional growth theory, the main determinants of long run economic growth are not influenced by economic incentives. Perhaps the reason why economists have neglected long time, to profession relied on a theory that offered litter scope for policy to influence important sources of growth.

Population growth technology

Some economists found one key is that education and anti-discrimination policies well designed labor market and large and/or progressive tax and transfer system can all reduce income inequality . In many OECD developed western countries, income inequality has increased in past decades. In some countries, top earners have captured a large share of overall income gains, when for other income has risen only a little. Some see poverty as the relevant concern with the type of growth enhancing policy reforms advocated for each OECD developed countries and economic growth might have positive or negative side effects on income inequality.

OECD (2011), it first highlights differences in some income inequality across the OECD and the factors driving them, such as cross-country differences in wage and non-wage income inequality as well as in hour worked and inactivity. OECD developed western countries can be divided into five groups to their pattern of inequality. For example, in five English-speaking countries (Australia, Canada, Ireland, New Zealand, the United Kingdom) and the Netherlands wages are rather dispersed and the share of part-time employment is high, driving inequality in labor earnings above the OECD average means-tested public cash transfer and progressive tax.

It seems income inequality will influence the developed countries, such as UK, Canada, Australia, New Zealand , US etc. economic growth. Although, technology change and globalization have played a role to influence the distribution of labor income. Some economists believe that any countries' policies will also influence income inequality. These policies factors include: technological education policies can increase different technology graduation rates from upper secondary and tertiary education and that also promote equal access to a well-designed different sector technology labor market policy can reduce inequality.

A relatively high minimum wage narrows the distribution if labor income, but if set too high, it may reduce employment of inequality reducing effect. It tends to reduce labor earning inequality by ensuring a more equal distribution of earnings. Job protection reforms that make permanent and temporary contracts more even in their provisions low income wage dispersion of earnings is rather mixed, removing product market regulations can reduce labor income inequality by boosting employment, policies the faster the immigrants and fight all forms of discrimination reduce inequality, progressive tax policy play a key role in lowering overall income across the OECD developed countries.

However, the redistributive fair income level between low level income labors and middle level income labors and high level income labors impact of developed countries, e.g. consumption taxes and real estate taxes tend to be regressive tax policy. Hence, it seems that reducing income inequality can cause the more fair income distribution between the high income level and the middle income level and the low income level labors. Then, it will let the developing countries or developed countries , such as US citizens feel that who can get real social welfare fairly, due to high technology development can boost economic growth in US society.

Cheap medical development technology

Some economists predict to make long term forecasts to reduce medical cost trends how will influence US economy. Also, they indicate short run cheap medical cost forecasts for first 1 to 5 years to reflect the particulars of specific groups, benefit packages, regional markets or cheap medical cost network providers and use their local cheap medical choice information and actuarial skills to improve accuracy and reasonability. They also oversight group review on the consistency of baseline assumptions with factor influencing future US patients' medical choice taste, medical technology trend component and historical annual percentage increase in medical costs, premiums, income and excess cost growth are found to influence future US patients consumption behavior. However, their research predicting expensive medical cost is the main factor to influence to reduce US patient numbers among of ward room sleeping environment, doctor loyalty, hospital entertainment and service facilities provision hospital cheap car parking charge service, cheap or free telephone call provision, hospital meal quality provision etc. different factors .

They suggest that how to reduce medical cost. They indicate many other factors, e.g. patient individual illness aging, physician supply, medical insurance plan benefit will affect the cost of a particular patient, group, organization or plan in a specific locality or over the short run. Also they indicated that additional analysis is still needed to determine if reliable estimates of separate medical insurance premiums, medical care payments, pharmaceuticals or other cost categories are possible to influence medical cost to be increase.

Hence, for long run US cheap medical cost will encourage or attract many patients prefer to pay medical cost to see doctors in US any hospitals or medical centers. Then, US hospitals or medical centers income will increase and US GDP income will also increase in medical service sectors in the future. It seems that long run cheap medical cost will influence US economic growth.

Artifical intelligent talent management technology

The next generation of US talent management practices and solutions will largely be driven by US economic evolution, demographic changes and technology advancements. These factors are dramatically influencing the way US people work, the way US companies are organized and the way talent is managed.

Some economists explained the key economic factors driving changes in talent management include: the knowledge economy is value to companies, talent is now a required strategic asset. Key changes in the future include a line between inside and outside talent that will result expansion of the talent management, globalization, such as European expansion is well-known top expansion prospect for global companies now include China, Russia and Eastern Europe and America and the rest of Asia. So , US government needs to know globalization can give what opportunities to US future .

Although, knowledge management or knowledge economy will bring advantages to US. However, it also bring disadvantages to this aspect, such as skill gap and structural unemployment will also influence US organizations structural unemployment and skill gap challenges issues will be caused between low skillful and high skillful workers, generational geographies changing will occur in US.

Although, baby boomer retirement has been top of mind for many years in the US, even more significant demographic changes are happening outside the US, where population growth rates and aging population will influence as local economies. Thus, the ability for organizations success will need global talent or effectively more talent from areas of abundance to scarcity is becoming a strategic issue to any US companies development , increased health and longevity mean that seniors are working longer enabling US organizations to keep experienced team members into their retirement years. But it also raise US workforce planning and generational challenges, workplace and diversity is increasing, a more diverse pool of talent affords new opportunity . Such as hiring workers raise productivity of needs, digitization of candidate or employee profiles can meet US business employment needs because employee talent data has been digitized and integrated into comprehensive talent profiles.

Techniques , such as attribute matching and recommendation technologies can be applied in talent management can be applied in talent management to find and match the most right candidate to do any positions in short time efficiently, with the increasing need of telecommunication in the US market penetration of smartphones and tablet devices a significant portion of the world's human potential will have access to rich web and application experiences from anywhere. Thus enables US organizations to source and collaborate on knowledge work with any part of the world into a global talent pool.

How can intellectual assets impact to US to change to knowledge economy? The information age moved the basis of economic value from products to intellectual assets, information and the talent that develops them. It is now widely acknowledged that intangible assets, with largely consist of know-how, unique intelligent property, and patent right, drive move than 80% of the valuations of publishing US publicly traded companies.

In future US knowledge economy, US leading edge organizations will have efforts to use into the talent and intellectual capital of not only employees, but also clients, partners and the public at large in an effort to create an extended electronic community. For example, client support portals where clients can answer each other's questions, which will reduce costs by expensive client support calls for US companies in future US knowledge economy environment.

Also, knowledge economy will assist US companies to be partner and customer innovation efforts easily. Such as P&G daily product company's ability to source more than 50% its new product ideas to external innovation, driving industry-leading standards for new product launch rates. In future knowledge economy environment, it is clear that US organizations will be increasingly deriving value from talent that is outside the company.

In future US knowledge economy environment, the link between employees within the US organization and those outside, it is also driving talent management changes, particularly around sourcing, strategic workforce planning and employees engagement . Given these changes, executives in leading US companies will be increasingly focused on talent management issues, recognizing that talent, wherever knowledge economy will give knowledge management method to any US organizations to build more competitive advantages in the future. However, knowledge economy will also bring structural unemployment to US society. Unfortunately, today's global talent market is largely inefficient and characterized by a high degree if competition relative to the redistribution of talent.

One result of this inefficiency is long period of skill gaps structured unemployment is a particularly different scenario in which section skills are no longer required, not just within a US particular company, but within US an entire sector. Structural unemployment may be the future result of cyclical boom and bust cycles, offshoring of partial. In conclusion, whatever the causes of future knowledge economy to US , the result is an uneven distribution of talent relative to the available jobs in US. In part of structured unemployment in US will be caused from knowledge economy influence. However, knowledge economy will also influence US future businesses speed increases, bandwidth increases and growth in mobile internet access during US encounters the knowledge economy influence in society.

Distance learning educational quality technology
Schools can train skills of an individual and human capital for future businessmen need. It is not the only factor. Schools nonetheless have a special place, not only because education and skill creation are among that prime explicit objectives, but also because which the factor(s) most directly are affected by public policies. So, US is well established that the distribution personal incomes in US society is strongly related to the amount of education US people have had. Thus, any noticeable effects of the current quality of US schooling and the distribution of US people skills and income will become apparent some years in the future, those US students now in US school become a significant part of the future US labor force. Then, the question arises as: To whether are these skills correlated with US student's subsequent performance in the future US labor market and will the US economy's ability to grow ?
The quality of human resources are measured by scores is directly related to individual earnings , productivity and economic growth. A range of research results from the United States shows that earnings advantages , due to higher achievement on standardized tests are quite substantial . These studies typically find that measured achievement has a clear impact on earnings, after allowing for a differences in the quantity of schooling, age or work experience, and for other factors that might influencing US people earnings. In other words, for those leaving school at a given grad, higher quality school outcomes (represented by test scores) are closely related to subsequent earnings differences. So, it seems quality of education and individual income has direct relationship to influence US economic growth.

According, educational program that deliver those skills will bring higher individual economic benefits. Obviously, students who don't better in schools as evidenced by either examination grades or scores on standardized achievement tests tend to go further in school or university. By the same way, the net costs of improvement in school quality if reduction in rates of student repetition study. Then, it brings this question: Will education quality bring future economic return to US?

Early some economists' research found that personal and behavioral traits, such as perseverance and leadership qualities had a significant influence upon labor market success, including earnings. To answer above question, we need to know if US schools which generally have good student performance, it will influence socio-economic advantage improved performance, changes in school climate, teacher morale and commitment, school autonomy , teacher-pupil relations and disciplinary had some compensatory influence towards greater equity. In American, pupil socio-economic background and classroom climate appeared to be the most important predictors of achievement. So, it seems human development will influence US economic growth in the future. So, US development organizations seem better will then non-specialized educational organizations to design and deliver effective combinations of livelihoods and literacy.

Whether people who attain literacy actually make much use of it is subject to debate. On balance, however, literacy seems more used where economic development is better established. This supports the argument that same degree of economic and political improvement is necessary to sustain literacy. Then, US people will use their literacy skills where conditions make it useful or desirable for them to do so. However, schooling is a social process, and improvements in resources, technology and quality of student and teaching inputs should in principle to able to be enhance its overall quality. In a good number of countries, large increases in average real expenditure per student and other measures of school resources in primary and secondary schools over the last four or five decades have not remotely been matched by a comparable increase in average test scores.

What can be influenced from quality of education to US? Some economists suggest the earning can provide an important incentive mechanism, which can influence both the quality and motivation of teachers. If teachers' real average earnings had kept the same level with other professional groups over the period, the productivity impact of their earnings growth would literacy have been small. The first view point, in fact, however, in many countries teachers' earnings have increased considerably less sharply than those other groups. Teachers may feel worse off, because of their decline in status relative to other professional groups. This circumstance could well explain part perhaps an important part of the apparent lack of impact on learning outcomes of increase in real per student spending over time. One to teachers' general salary is low to compare other professional in the global society.

Then, it brings this question. Can quantity of education influence US economic growth? In this modern economic approach to investigating the determinants of educational outcomes has borrowed well established technique from other economic applications. The idea that there is a determinate relationship between (teacher number) inputs to a production process (teaching process) and the outputs(student examination results and learning performance) that subsequently bring has being been important in micro-economic analysis. If US schooling teaching possibilities are governed by certain teachers' quality between factors of production, e.g. teachers; teaching performance , teachers' supply numbers to every schools, teachers' educational qualification. So, the product function describes the maximum feasible output (student examination results and learning combinations) obtained from alternative combinations of these inputs (teachers' quality teaching performance, supply numbers, education qualification).

Production factors are powerful analytic tools, which have been applied to the analysis of most forms of economic production. Since the mid-1960 year, they have also been widely used in the economic analysis of education. Thus, in schooling educational organizations, teacher salaries will influence teachers' performance (production of factor) to be good or bad. If teachers' educational performance is good, then production of output (student learning abilities and students examination results) will be good usually. Otherwise, if their educational performance is bad, then production of output (student learning abilities and students examination results) will be bad usually .

In US society, if many poor learning performance students have been produced. Then, there will not many talent young people who can contribute to serve US society in different professional aspects. It means that they can not contribute US economic growth easily. Thus, it seems that US quality of education can impact US economic growth for long term and US universities, secondary schools and US government ought need to find methods how to raise quality of education for next generation of labor supply market.

Bio-medical technology

In the future, the perspective of bio-medical industry will be an alternative growth scenario. So, US government will need to modest improvements in key policy areas to adopt bio-medical industry needs, e.g. more favorable coverage and payment policies for medical innovation, improvements in regulatory policy to create efficiencies in research and development process and improvements in policy to incentive R & D (research and development) create efficiencies in the R & D process.

As an industry rooted in science and advanced manufacturing, the innovation bio-medical industry is uniquely position to help maintain US leadership in new technologies and scientific to continue to create high quality, high wage R&D and manufacturing jobs and enhance America's global competitiveness in the future. Today, the US bio-medical industry supports a total of 3.4 million jobs across the US economy , including over 810,000 direct jobs: contributes $189 billion in economic output and is responsible for about one in five dollars spent on domestic R&D by US businesses. Hence, innovation bio-medical industry will be one high value knowledge-based industries as a driver of US economic growth.

The reasons include: The first reason is such as , the US history, it has been the world leader in bio-medical research and development of new medicine over the past 30 years. It has been one leader of world class life science ecosystem and innovation among different countries in medicine development history. So, bio-medical industry will be a high technological innovation related activity of industry leader, as is measured by R&D investment, e.g. generation venture capital and share a total R&D employment in manufacturing industry. Next reason is that US bio-medical industry employs a total of 813, 523 worker amount. These workers lead a wide range of occupations that offer high wage, high quality employment. The total economic impacts of the industry, it is estimated (via the generally accepted methodology of input/output analysis) that supports nearly 3.4 million total jobs and generates nearly $ 789 billion in US economic output (National Science Board, 2014). Finally, reason is that US people concern life health issue, In addition to improving individual health and lengthening life ages, medical advances have contributed to substantial societal health gains, such as reducing disability and improving productivity.

According to two Universities of Chicago economists indicated the estimated economic gains from declining morality alone in the US from 1970 year to 2000 year had a value to US society of more than 3 trillion a year. Hence, US medical health need of patient numbers will increase, due to who have large needs for life health. Hence, quality of education can influence bio-medical industry development to impact US economic growth in the future.

Influencing future UK and US
technological development factors

Welfare economic theory, Kaldor-Hicks efficiency theory and Pareto improvement theory relationship

Economists explain that welfare economic theory, Kaldor-Hicks efficiency theory and Pareto improvement theory which have close relationship. Welfare economic theory means general social equilibrium. They indicate the demand of commodities must same to the supply of commodities when the commodity market stays in the stable level. So , when production is increasing, the manufacturers also need to keep their products supply and demand keep to the stable level and consumers' demand of their products must also need to increase as well as bank interest rate must be fallen in order to raise consumption desires. Also, the low bank interest can also excite investors' investment desires.

Such as to explain why the developing countries cities technological competitive investment factor can impact US and UK economic growth. Welfare economic theory means general social equilibrium. The economists indicate the demand of commodities must same to the supply of commodities when the commodity market stays in the stable level. Due to the future developing countries investors will invest much on developing new technological products research. So, these countries' economy growth will be possible faster than US and UK both developed countries because it is possible that the technological product investor number will decrease. So, US and UK government will need to attract and encourage many foreign developing countries' investor prefer to invest their technological products research to assist US and UK both developed countries to develop its economy. As Welfare economic theory means general social equilibrium. If US and UK government can give benefits to these developing countries' technological product investors, then these developing countries' technological product investors will prefer to invest to developed country US urban cities, such as small cities or farming location to build factories to manufacture their new technological products. Because , London, New York, Washington etc. large cities' technological investment and location where land supply is limited and offices and factories rents are also expensive. Otherwise, UK and US, farming location or small cities location where have much land supply to build large offices and facilities and the rent is much cheaper than US and UK main cities, such as London, New York, Washington etc. Even, if UK and US government and banks can lend low interest rate of bank loans or government loans to encourage foreign investors to do technological product research in its country. So, UK and US bank low bank interest rate can encourage US consumers prefer to buy any future new technological products, due to low bank interest rate can not attract who choose to save more money in US and UK any banks as well as US and UK bank low bank interest rate can also encourage foreign developing countries' high technological product investors to choose to invest in UK and UK , due to who can pay low bank or government loan interest to compare themselves countries or other countries.

As Kaldor-Hicks efficiency theory indicates the policy is suitable to be implemented if the policy beneficiaries' welfares can compensate to the policy benefactress. So, US and UK bank and government low loan interest rate policy is valuable to implement if benefactress, such as US and UK government which can raise economic growth as well as the US benefactress, such as the high technological product businessmen can sell many different kinds of high technological products from foreign developing countries' investors' assistance in US and UK both developed countries.

As Pareto improvement theory indicates that it can not carry on continue, due to the country has shortage of natural resources after the country improved its welfares to reach the maximum standard. The result will be caused, such as the country will reduce this group of citizen's welfares, if the country decides to continue to improve another group of citizen's welfares. So, future US and UK will have shortage of natural resources to supply to technological product manufacturers. So, the number of technological product production will be fallen , due to the shortage of natural resources are supplied to US and UK high technological product manufacturers. The only solvable choice is encouraging foreign high technological product investors to attract them to supply themselves high technological products any resources to manufacture high technological products and provide to US and UK high technological product sellers to help them to sell in US and UK domestic market or export to overseas market to earn income. Then, US and UK will earn raise GDP income from high technological product sale industry in the future.

Natural rate of unemployment factor

Economists believe why natural rate of unemployment will occur in any countries. They indicate that during economy condition keeps at the balance situation (condition), anyway any country government adopts any policy. However, the natural rate of unemployment won't reach to zero level as well as there are some people will still unemployed or it is possible that some people will be alternative employment between any time. Hence, it means that although US and UK is an developed country. It can not guarantee there are not any people unemployed , so the natural rate of unemployment will not reach to zero level.

So, it seems that US and UK current economy condition had kept at the balance situation (condition). Thus, even future science, technology , engineering and mathematics workers will drive US innovation and competitiveness by new ideas, new companies and new industries in US. However, US and UK employers frequently concern the supply and availability of this kind of workers. Over the past 10 years, growth in this kind of jobs was three times as fast as growth to general jobs in US. In the future the Natural rate of unemployment of US and UK science, technology , engineering and mathematics worker number must not reach zero level.

Anyway, in the future, the perspective of bio-medical industry will be an alternative growth scenario. So, US and UK government will need to modest improvements in key policy areas to adopt bio-medical industry needs, e.g. more favorable coverage and payment policies for medical innovation, improvements in regulatory policy to create efficiencies in research and development process and improvements in policy to incentive R & D (research and development) create efficiencies in the R & D process.

As an industry rooted in science and advanced manufacturing, the innovation bio-medical industry is uniquely position to help maintain US leadership in new technologies and scientific to continue to create high quality, high wage R&D and manufacturing jobs and enhance America's global competitiveness in the future. In the future the Natural rate of unemployment of US and UK of bio-medical industry worker number must not reach zero level.

Thus, if future US had enough job number which could supply to these high technological and bio medical industries of labors to do. However, the natural rate of unemployment must not reach at zero level and it does not represent its economy is poor because one developed country , such as US had been experiencing economy condition keeps at the balance situation(condition), so it's natural rate of unemployment must not reach zero level . Otherwise, the developing countries' economy condition does not keep at the balance situation (condition), so their natural rate of unemployment have more possible to reach to close zero level.

Industrial production and pollution economic factor

Economists indicate that it has close relationship between industrial production and pollution. When traditional products are manufactured, the air and water pollution will be caused in the economic activity. So, human needs to protect environment to keep health, the demand of investment of money reduces pollution and labor number will increase to achieve to reduce air and water pollution in natural environment. Thus, product manufacturers need to analyze which economic stage(s) will encounter shortage and find methods to solve challenge.

This Industrial production and pollution economy theory can explain why US and UK needs to plan achieve digital economy to shift future America rural economy. Some economists indicate that there are five trends reshape to impact rural America' and England future economy. They include that digital economy will shift future America rural economy. US and UK quality of life will change a lot, the US and UK rural economy will stay uneven, US commodities will compete in global markets and will give less benefit to US and UK rural economy and US and UK new products will revolutionize US and UK agriculture economy.

US and UK needs to plan digital economy to future agricultural production of the reasons include: The first aspect impacts to US agriculture economy, the US future rural economy stays uneven. Growth will concentrate in 4 out of 10 rural places and they have scenery, a retail hub, or one next to a city in US and UK. The impact on rural America includes some rural places will try to manage growth , but many places on a quest for new economic engines. Thus, it will bring these questions to US and UK rural economy impact, such as : Who will be US and UK businessmen clients? The struggling farmers?

The struggling farm-dependent country? The booming mountain area? The rural area transforming into city? The second aspect impacts to US and UK agriculture economy, due to US and UK commodities will compete in global markets if it will bring a smaller benefit in US and UK rural economy. Then, US and UK farm scale will cut costs and competition fewer US and UK farms and places will depend on farm income. The third aspect impact to US and UK agriculture economy, new products will revolutionize agriculture. Major, shift from commodities to products, spurred by biotech, means two agriculture in the future and two rural America . Hence, US and UK future agriculture determination the rural economy will be declined. A future new US and UK agriculture supply chain integrator will be caused from the traditional farming supply chain procedure the change to outsourced contractor farming supply chain procedure, such as: In beginning, from farmer will outsource supply chain contract to processor, then contract to distributor and contract to food retailer final step. The fourth aspect impacts to US and UK agriculture economy, what will be two agricultures impact to the US and UK future economy? The first US and UK agriculture impact will be US and UK commodity agriculture. It focuses on production capabilities, farming foods production will be thin margins maintained with technology and big sale. The second US and UK agriculture impact will be product agriculture. It focuses on consumer needs, farming foods production margins will be protected by capturing value and building business relationship. In the fifth aspect impacts to US and UK agricultural economy, it is digital economy impacts US and UK rural agriculture. Future diversity economic base can encourage US and UK farming product agriculture to enter rural digital agricultural service consumption sector to change US and UK agricultural consumer individual shopping habit.

Thus, future US and UK agricultural production needs to concern how to reduce air and water pollution to influence natural environment clean quality as well as it needs to find what economic stage of agricultural production will be innovated in the future.

Reference

Akerlof, G.A. & Kranton, R.E. (2000): Economics & Identity, Quarterly Journal Of Economics, 105(3) , 715-753.

Barro, R., Sala-i-Martin, X., (1996). The classical approach to convergence analysis. The economic journal, vol. 106, no. 437.

Bernard, A., Redding, S & Schott, P. (2006). " Multi- product firms and product switching, " NBER working paper, 12293.

Bloom, D., Canning, D., Sevilla, J., 2001. Economic growth and demographic transition. National Bureau Of Economic Research.

Brynjolfsson and Mc Afee, (2011). Race against the machine: how the digital revolution is accelerating innovation and driving productivity , US.

Bresnahan, T.T. (1999). computerisation and wage dispersion: an analytical reinterpretation. The economic journal, vol. 109, no. 456 pp. 390-415.

David. M Gould & Roy. J. Ruffin. What determines long run economy growth? Economic review, second quarter, 1993.

ESA (2010 & 2018 year) calculations using current population survey public use micro date and estimates from the employment projections program of those Bureau of labor statistics.

Fernald, John (2015). " Productivity snd potential output before during, and after the great recession" In Jonathan A Parker & Michael

Hakkio, Craig S. 1992. " Is purchasing power parity a useful guide to the dollar?" Federal reserve bank of Kansas city, Economic review, third quarter, pp. 37-51.

Harrison, Huntington, S . (2000). Culture matters: how values shape human progess. Basic books.

John, G. 2016 " Reassessing longer run US growth. How low? " Federal reserve bank of San Francisco working paper 2016-18. http://www.frbsf.org/economic-research/publications/working-papers/ wp2016-18/pdf.

Martin, J.P. & S. Scarpetta. " Setting it right. employment protection, labor reallocation and productivity." De Economist , 60: 2 (2012): 89-116. Online at: http://ideas. repec.org/p/iza/izapps/pp.27 html (3).

MGI (2013). Disruptive technologies: Advances that will transform life business and the global economy. Tech. Rep: Mckinsey Global Institute.

National Science Board, 2014 , Science and Engineering Indicators, USP TO Patent applications and grants by industry.

OECD (2011), Divided We Stand: Why Inequality Keeps Rising, OECD publishing.

US Travel Association " US Travel Employment Reaches An Time high" (press release) , Nov. 7, 2014 Accessed Dec. 8 , 2014. available here :   http://www.ustravel.org/news/press-releases/travel-industry-employment-reaches-all-time-high.

US Bureau of the census, 1993. Statistical abstract of the United States, 113 the ed. Washington.

CHAPTER FOUR

www.ingramcontent.com/pod-product-compliance
Lightning Source LLC
Chambersburg PA
CBHW071338150726
47997CB00002B/782